RICHARD OF LINCOLN

A Medieval Doctor Travels to Jerusalem

Edited and Translated

by

Francis Davey

Azure Publications

Published by Azure Publications
Burraton Bungalow, Broadclyst, Exeter EX5 3DB

Printed by Short Run Press Ltd, Bittern Road
Sowton Industrial Estate, Exeter EX2 7LW

First printed June 2013

ISBN 978-0-9569346-1-1

Any profits from the sale of this book will be given to The Wellcome Library

Cover illustrations from: Konrad von Grünenberg; *Beschreibung der Reise von Konstanz nach Jerusalem*

CONTENTS

Part 1. Introduction: the Doctor and the Priest

Part 2. The Text

Part 3. Translation of the Text

Part 4. Notes on the Text

Part 5. Bibliography

Part 6. Index

.-.-.-.-.-.-.-.-.-.-.-.-.-.-.-.-.-.-.

Key:

D - Dover
G - Ghent
C - Cologne
S - Strasbourg
B - Basle
M - Milan
V - Venice
R - Ragusa
Me - Methoni
Ca - Candia
Rh - Rhodes
P - Paphos
J - Jaffa

The Journey from Dover to Jerusalem

© Daniel Dalet / d-maps.com

Preface

Thirty-four men and women gathered in the Tabard Inn in Southwark on an April day towards the end of the 14th century, 'on pilgrimage to go'. Their goal was Canterbury, but there were others whose aim was 'seeking distant shrines renowned in sundry lands'. In the next century, two of these, Richard, a doctor, and William, a priest, travelled to Jerusalem and left factual accounts of their journeys. These were rather less colourful than the tales collected by Geoffrey Chaucer, but not devoid of interest. Richard of Lincoln left Dover in 1454 and William Wey sailed from Gravesend eight years later.

My wife and I have spent most of our holidays since retirement following William's and Richard's routes across Europe and beyond. In producing this book I wish to acknowledge my debt to the institutions and people who have made it possible.

At the beginning, chance or serendipity played a major part in the endeavour to come. One Sunday morning, I woke with a start as I heard the word 'pilgrimage' on Radio Four's *Sunday* programme. The voice was that of the medieval historian, Diana Webb, being interviewed about the recent acquisition of the Richard of Lincoln manuscript by the Wellcome Library. Her enthusiasm was contagious and being already well acquainted with William Wey through his Bodleian Library manuscript and 19th-century transcription, I decided that Richard must be followed up in similar fashion.

Since then, the support and interest of my wife, Patricia Quaife, have been unfailing, and as noted in my book on William Wey's *Itineraries* (Bodleian Library, 2010) she has 'shared our quest across land, sea and time'. Second, the Wellcome Library, which kindly gave me my first chance to see Richard's manuscript just as they acquired it, has now given its permission for it to be used in this book. Finally, I am deeply grateful to Robin and Diane Wilks of Azure Publications, Exeter, whose encouragement, assistance and computer skills could not have been more generously offered. Without them my research would never have seen the light of day. I offer my deep thanks to all of them.

Francis Davey
March 2013

3

PART 1

The Doctor and the Priest

Introduction   5

The Routes:
   1. England to Venice   6
   2. Venice to Jaffa   9
   3. The Holy Land   11
   4. Homeward Bound   13
   5. Money, Transport and Accommodation   13
   6. Conclusion   16

Appendix   16

Two Fifteenth-Century English Pilgrims to Jerusalem

Who that will to Jerusalem go must make his change at London with the Lombards.

With these words a fifteenth-century physician of Lincoln began the account of his pilgrimage to the Holy Land.

In April 2002, the then Arts Minister, Baroness Blackstone, placed a temporary bar on the export of an important medieval manuscript which a rare books dealer was planning to send abroad. This manuscript, now commonly known as *The Physician's Handbook* by "Richard of Lincoln", was formerly in the library of the Dukes of Newcastle at Clumber Park, Notts. until that collection was dispersed in 1938. The Minister's intervention enabled the Wellcome Trust to purchase the manuscript which is now MS 8004 in the Wellcome Library for the History and Understanding of Medicine, and may be viewed on the Internet.

This book is an English medical and astrological compendium of about 100 leaves written in the middle of the fifteenth century. The introduction to the calendar which opens the book states that it was begun in 1454. Apart from astrological and calendar tables the book contains two striking, coloured anatomical drawings. That of "Zodiac man" illustrates the special relationship which was thought to exist between the signs of the Zodiac and various human limbs and organs, while the other picture shows the location of 24 veins and the physical or mental conditions which indicate they should be opened.

Apart from practising his profession Richard went on pilgrimage to Jerusalem, and incorporates an account of his travels in *The Physician's Handbook.* If, as seems likely, he made his visit in 1454, he made it only four years before William Wey, priest, sometime Fellow of Exeter College, Oxford and Fellow and Bursar of Eton College, made his first visit to the Holy Land. William Wey's description of his three pilgrimages (to Compostella in 1456, to Rome and Jerusalem in 1458 and to Jerusalem again in 1462) is to be found in his *Itineraries,* preserved in the Bodleian Library (MS 565). The present author's translation and edition of Wey's book was published by the Bodleian Library in 2010 (ISBN 978 1 85124 3044). Since each of these pilgrims left a written account of his journey it is most interesting to compare them. The two men covered much of the same ground and at much the same time and so, predictably, there are many similarities between their observations, but, since one was a layman and the other a priest, although both were making the pilgrimage for reasons of piety, their interests and backgrounds lead to different emphases and attitudes.

Richard's account forms about a tenth of *The Physician's Handbook* (folios 75r to 83v) and is written in a fifteenth-century dialect known as Danelaw Middle English. (I am grateful to Professor Linda Voigts of the University of Missouri for this ascription.) He uses a mere handful of Latin words or abbreviations, e.g. *flum. Jordan* (the River Jordan), and *Mar. Morte* (the Dead Sea), *Porta Aurea* (the Golden Gate), *Probatica Piscina* (the Pool of Sheep; i.e. Bethesda; see St John 5, 2-4) and *a poena et culpa* (from punishment and sin).

William Wey's *Itineraries* is a very much more substantial work, running to 104 folios, i.e. more than ten times the length of Richard's pilgrimage account. It contains 15 "chapters", the first three in English followed by 12 in Latin. The journeys are described in Chapter 7 (Rome and Jerusalem), Chapter 9 (Jerusalem) and Chapter 15 (Compostella). To these should be added Chapter 8, which is simply a list of places and the distances between them, en route from Calais to Venice via Rome and from Venice back to Calais, and Chapter 14, which is a description of churches, relics and indulgences to be found in Rome. Chapter 8 has special significance since both men followed the same route from England almost to the Rhine. Wey's other chapters include much interesting material. Chapters 5 and 6, for instance, investigate motives for pilgrimage, while Chapter 10 consists of several vocabularies: English-Greek, Greek-Latin and Latin-Hebrew. Chapter 11 is a sort of common-place notebook with fascinating facts and anecdotes which Wey did not find room for in the final versions of his pilgrimage narratives. Beginning with a brief history of Venice and her maritime empire he then lists sacred sites on the way to the Holy Land. There is part of an alleged letter from Saladin to the Master of the Knights Hospitaller, stories of St George and other saints and much else. Chapters 12 and 13 are topographical, being lists of places and distances designed to accompany his *Mappa Terrae Sanctae* which is also in the Bodleian (MS Douce 389).

THE ROUTES

1. England to Venice

Richard travelled from Dover via Calais, Gravelines, Dunkirk, Newport, Bruges, Ghent, Dendermonde, Mechelen, Aarschot, Diest, Hasselt, Maastricht and Aachen to Cologne. From Cologne he followed the Rhine upstream to Bonn, Remagen, Andernach, Coblenz, Boppard, Bacharach, Bingen, Mainz, Worms, Speyer, Strasburg and Basel. Thence he went via Lucerne, Flüelen and Wasen to the Saint Gotthard. From Faido he passed through Bellinzona, Lugano, Como, Milan and Pavia. From Pavia he went down the Po to Cremona and so to Venice "all by water".

William, in 1458, followed the same route as Richard from Calais to Aachen. His list of "staging points" is almost identical, and, as one would expect, the distances between them, given by each man, vary only very slightly.

Both pilgrims are conscious of the variety of "miles" in use along the way. While Wey only tells us where "Italian miles start", e.g. at Ala, Richard is most particular in saying, first, where Flemish miles start; i.e. at Calais, - "a Flemish mile is three English miles". He next states that Dutch miles commence at Maastricht, and "in Lower Germany a Dutch mile is four English miles". After Basel there is a different "Dutch mile, which is six English miles". Finally in Lombardy, (after Göschenen), "three Lombardy miles make two English miles".

After Aachen, Wey, who in 1458 was going south to Rome before travelling northwards to Venice to join the pilgrim galley, took a slightly different route to reach the Rhine. He joined this river near Andernach and then followed it, like Richard, as far as Speyer. After Speyer, however, Wey took a very different route, via Ulm and Memmingen, to Kempten, Merano, Trento, Florence and Siena to Rome.

In 1462 William Wey sailed from Gravesend to Annemuiden and continued by sea to Antwerp. From there he again passed through Maastricht and Aachen but then, "because of a war between two bishops", he had to make a detour turning south to pass through Trier.

Keeping well to the west of the Rhine he made his way from Trier to Metz, along the Moselle, and so to Basel. Here too hostilities caused a change of route. This time it was a war between Pope Pius and the Duke of Austria, and the Pope had threatened to excommunicate any person who crossed the Duke's territory. In Chapter 9 Wey describes the longer route which he followed, together with his friends, - both like him, being priests and also called "William". They went via Konstanz, Landeck and Merano, probably using the old *Via Julia Claudia*, to Trento, Padua and Venice, where they arrived on 22nd April, 1462.

Here one may point out an important difference between the accounts given by Richard and William. Richard gives no information about the exact dates when his pilgrimage began and ended. It is only his mention of "the General Council of all clergy of Christendom", held at Basel, which gives us a *terminus post quem* for the date of his pilgrimage. The Council was held at Basel until 1448, being then moved to Lausanne where it came to an end in the following year. In contrast, Wey gives such detailed information about his dates and times that it is possible to reconstruct a virtual diary for his travels to Compostella, Rome and Jerusalem.

Medieval pilgrims to the great shrines of Christendom, in Jerusalem, Rome or Compostella, where important indulgences were available for the faithful, were well aware of other pilgrimage sites which lay on or near their routes and could confer spiritual benefits. While some persons, e.g. parish clergy or royal servants, whose licence from their superiors to travel on pilgrimage specified the length of time they could be absent from their duties, did have to take account of the amount of time they could spend on detours, for many the length of time spent on the pilgrimage was not a pressing consideration. In these cases detours were devoutly made and the additional indulgences gladly accepted. Both Richard and William were well aware of these further opportunities and the extra shrines and relics they mention are tabulated below in the Appendices.

When Wey describes the service at Pergine in northern Italy, which he attended on Good Friday, 16th April, in 1462, he gives us the tiniest glimpse of his companions, describing them as two priests also called William. In the 1458 account, in Chapter 7, Wey several times mentions the name of another of his fellow-pilgrims, John Tiptoft, the Earl of Worcester, who was on pilgrimage with a large retinue of servants and musicians. We know from other sources the names of several other pilgrims in this year, (see *The Spring Voyage* by RJ Mitchell, London 1965), but Wey himself is not very forthcoming in this area. Perhaps the most poignant episode in *The Itineraries* is when Wey describes the rigours of the visit to Jordan. At the end of this paragraph he writes, "After visiting these sites we arrived that night at Jericho, where we lay for four hours on the stones. A French priest died that night and was buried halfway along the road from Jerusalem to Jericho." Details of this nature are not found in Richard's account. He gives no indication whether he was travelling to Venice alone or with friends. Once at Venice, however, he would have had companions willy-nilly. Usually, at this period, two pilgrim galleys set sail from Venice for the Holy Land each year. They left Venice round about the third week in May when the north-west wind known as the *Maestro* or *Maestrale* starts to blow and gives vessels sailing southwards down the Dalmatian coast welcome assistance. Each galley carried about 100 pilgrims, but Richard does not mention this.

Both pilgrims give information about the sailing arrangements which must be made at

Venice. Richard's account is very short, "At Venice a man must take his galley. And a man must pay for his passage within the galley as the patron and he may accord. And the most that any man pay is 16, or 40 ducats and to be at the patron's board, and the bed will cost ye another ducat and a half." William, on the other hand, devotes the whole of Chapter 2, "*A Provision*", to the arrangements which must be made with the patron. The fare is the same, 40 ducats, - "if you are going to get a good place and be comfortable in the galley and be well looked after … and for your meat and drink to the port of Jaffa and back to Venice." But then William Wey goes on to give details of the route, the distances between ports and the conditions of carriage which are part of the contract between pilgrim and patron. Next he offers very detailed, not to say homely, advice about the kit, provisions, condiments and medications which the pilgrim should purchase in Venice for himself and his servant "if you have one". All this information is given in English in Chapter 2 and again in Latin in the course of Chapter 9. Two examples may be given from this latter chapter of Wey's solicitude and the amount of detail he gives.

"You should also buy in Venice a small chamber pot, because if you become ill and are unable to climb up to the upper parts of the galley, you will be able to do what you have to in it."

And

"You can also buy a set of bed-clothes in Venice near St Mark's. For three ducats you will get a feather bed, a mattress, two pillows, two pairs of small linen sheets and a small quilt. When you return to the seller in Venice he will take them back and give you one and a half ducats for the set of bedding."

Richard's account of his progress through northern Europe is terse in the extreme. His vocabulary is small and his narrative consists mainly of the distances between successive stages on the route and the tolls and charges which the pilgrim must pay. He recognises only three categories of settlement, - villages, towns and cities. There are 11 in this last group, viz. Ghent, Cologne, Koblenz, Mainz, Worms, Speyer, Strasburg, Basel, Piacenza, Chioggia and Venice. The range of epithets is tiny; the only adjectives used for towns and cities are "walled", "little walled" or "full fair walled". Apart from villages, towns and cities the principal features Richard mentions are bridges, ferries and castles. The six bridges he names attract slightly more varied descriptions. The bridges at Maastricht and Pavia are "stone", that at Koblenz "fair stone", that at Basel "great" and that at "Thrusse" fair. The one at Lucerne, however, excited his admiration. He describes it as, "A fair, long timber bridge, roofed with tile. It is eight paces broad and half a mile long!".

Despite his brevity there are a few intriguing vignettes which include , "a good bating-house (a sort of medieval transport café) between Worms and Speyer", the fearsome legends surrounding Pilatus Lake near Lucerne, where Pontius Pilate is said to have drowned himself in remorse, a well at Pavia "that healeth of divers sickness both the man and the woman," (this well, later visited among others by François I, can still be seen in the crypt of San Andrea) and between Milan and Pavia, "a fair park, well-walled with tile, and therein be leopards and lions and all manner of other deer and marvellous manner of fowls; today this is the World Heritage Site of the *Certosa di Pavia*.

In his 1458 account (Chapter 7) William Wey says absolutely nothing about his journey until his arrival in Venice. In Chaper 8, which deals with the same journey and lists the distances between the stages on his route from England to Rome, thence to Venice and back to

England, he gives 16 tiny marginal notes indicating frontiers, places to change money, places where the length of a mile altered, the location of Universities (Bologna and Perugia) and the resting places of St Christina (Spoleto) and St Francis and St Clare (Assisi).

In Chapter 9, the 1462 pilgrimage, Wey is much more forthcoming. He explains why two detours had to be made (see above). He gives several interesting facts about Trier where there is a tomb of St Mathias, the well where Athanasius composed his Creed, the *Quicunque Vult*, and the knife used by St Peter when he cut off Malchas's ear. "In the church of St Mathias there are as many saints' bodies as there are days in the year" and "the Bishop of this city is one of those who elects the Emperor of Germany, who will be chosen in the city of Aachen." At the town of St Nicholas in Gaul "there is an arm of St Nicholas and the largest collection of chains and fetters I have ever seen in any church". Finally, in Northern Italy, as mentioned earlier, William and his two friends stayed in Pergine from Good Friday until Easter Monday, where they were hospitably received by the parish priest and assisted at an interesting service with a girls' choir on Easter Day.

Wey arrived in Venice on 22nd April and had five weeks to explore the city before embarking with the other pilgrims on their galley, the *Morosina*, on the 26th May. The vessel then moved to the traditional departure point, "The Towers of Venice", near St Nicholas Church, finally departing for Istria on 1st June.

As one would expect, the two men have their own interests which produce differences of emphasis. Wey was so impressed by Venice that he devotes approximately half of his Chapter 9 to a description of the city, its history and its ceremonies. The fact that he stayed there for five weeks during which time he witnessed three splendid events, namely the Doge's procession on St Mark's Day, the funeral of Doge Pascale Malopero and the coronation of the new Doge, Christophero Mauro, goes some way to explaining this. As a priest, Wey had a special interest in the clerical hierarchy, in vestments and processions. The colour and splendour of the ceremonies he saw shine through his narrative and he presents a detailed verbal description of the scene later depicted by Gentile Bellini in his work, now in the Accademia in Venice, *Procession in St Mark's Square*. Bellini painted this in 1496, but the events shown occurred on St Mark's Day in 1444. Wey's account describes the scene admirably. He was also interested in the way Venice was governed and he gives much detail about the city's complicated constitution and also its *Scuole*. While both men list the more important relics which can be seen in the city, Richard's description of the *Serenissima* is, in his usual, laconic way, simply, "Venice, a full fair city, standeth all in the sea."

2. Venice to Jaffa

Both Richard and William (in 1458) cover the voyage from Venice to Jaffa in just over a page. (For clarity, place-names are here again given in their modern forms.) Richard mentions Rovinj, Pula, Zadar, Korčula, Dubrovnik, Durres, Cassiopi, Corfu, Methoni, Candia (Herakleion), Rhodes and Jaffa. Wey's 1458 list runs: Poreč, Dubrovnik, Durres, Cassiopi, Corfu, Candia, Rhodes, Paphos and Jaffa. In 1462 Wey gives Poreč, Rovinj, Zadar, Sesule, Korčula, Dubrovnik, Corfu, Axtis (Methoni), Rhodes, Paphos and Jaffa. Again the distances given by each are very similar, in fact they are identical for the 1,600-mile voyage from Corfu to Jaffa, apart from the fact that Richard does not mention Cyprus by name. Perhaps they are taken from a "master copy" kept in Venice, which Wey uses in his Chapter 2 in English and in his Chapter 9 in Latin. We know from the Venetian state archives that the pilgrim trade was strictly regulated by the city authorities who were punctilious in ensuring that the interests of both pilgrims and the *patroni*, who owned the galleys and travelled on them, were properly protected. Wey writes in Chapter 2:-

"When you make the contract ensure that the *patron* is bound to you in the presence of the Doge or Lords of Venice in the sum of 100 ducats to observe in full the agreement with you; namely… that he will take you to Pula, 100 miles by water from Venice; from Pula to Corfu 600 miles; from Corfu to Modyn (Methoni) 300 miles; from Modyn to Cande 300 miles; from Cande to Rhodes 300 miles; from Rhodes to Baffa (Paphos) in Cyprus 400 miles; and from Baffa to Port Jaffa 300 miles."

Richard's stages are:- "From Venice 100 miles to Rovinj and 20 miles to Pula. From Pula 150 miles (to) Zadar. From Zadar 100 miles to (*gap*) and 50 miles to Korčula. And 100 miles to Ragusa (Dubrovnik). And 140 miles to Durres and 140 miles to Corfu. And from yonder to Methoni 300 miles and from Methoni 300 miles to Cande and 300 miles to Rhodes. And from Rhodes 700 miles to Port Jaffa, and ye are then in the Holy Land."

Both pilgrims mention St Euphemia at Rovinj and St Simeon, St Zoyolus and St Anastasia at Zadar. St Anastasia, a fourth-century saint, had her Feast Day on December 25th, which led Richard of Lincoln to state, incorrectly, that she was present at the birth of Christ. William Wey is more accurate, writing, "She is remembered on the day of Our Lord's Nativity because on that day she endured martyrdom by burning".

Both travellers were impressed by the wealth of Dubrovnik:-

"And 100 miles to Ragusa, a fair little walled town and a rich one." (RL)
and, "On the 24th May I came to the city of Ragusa. In that city is an arm of St Blaise, bishop. It is a wealthy city set on the coast with a fine wall. The silver money there is very good." (WW)

Both men, also, were intrigued by the miracle of the lamp in the chapel of the Blessed Virgin Mary at Casope, on the north-east coast of Corfu island facing Albania.

"And there is between Durres and Corfu a chapel which is called Casopa. And there ye shall hear a miracle, for there is a little lamp which burneth both night and day. And it is but once filled in the year." (RL)
and, "Next I came to Casope, a city which had been destroyed by a crocodile. There is a chapel of the Most Blessed Virgin Mary there where a lamp burns for one year on one filling of oil." (WW)

Richard's description of the voyage from Venice to Jaffa is as brief as the rest of his narrative. He does mention, however, two sites in Istria, near Pula, which legend connected with Roland. (Further south a medieval statue of Roland can still be seen in the square in Dubrovnik outside St Blaise's church. Although this was erected in 1418 neither pilgrim mentions it.)

William's 1458 account is almost as concise as Richard's, but that for 1462 is much more informative. He mentions the wine which can be bought at Lysme (Hvar), "where one can get more strong wine for one *grosset* than one can buy for eight in Venice," and Axtis (Methoni) "where the wine called *Romney* grows". Once in Rhodes, Wey's narrative expands greatly. Apart from listing the relics owned by the Knights Hospitaller, which are also, very briefly, described by Richard, he gives a most detailed account of the way in which the thorn from Christ's crown flowers and withers on Good Friday. There is a description of the seven islands near Rhodes owned by the Knights and the legends connected with them. A mention of the great Hospital on Rhodes leads him to describe the garrison in the castle of *Sympere*, i.e. St Pierre, at Bodrum, with its vigilant guard dogs, which patrol at night and "which are well able to distinguish Christian from Turk". The shadow of the Turks is always present in Wey's descriptions of the Eastern Mediterranean. Quite apart from the mutual hostility between them and the Knights Hospitaller, which led both sides to commit acts of chilling barbarity on their prisoners, the political situation in Cyprus, where the "bastard" King James usurped the rightful heir, his half-sister, Charlotte, with the help of the Saracen Sultan in Cairo, made travel between Rhodes and the Holy Land very dangerous. That they completed their pilgrimages during this decade is a tribute to the courage and devotion of both Richard and William and the other pilgrims who ventured thus far east. Constantinople had fallen in 1453, the Turks had forcibly transported 30,000 men, women and children from the Morea to repopulate it and Count Flad V of Wallachia, known to history as Vlad the Impaler, was fighting the Turks in a campaign which culminated in a massacre on Corpus Christi Day, 1462, of, so it was said, 30,000 Turks.

3. The Holy Land

As one would expect, there are many similarities between the accounts given by Richard and William of their tours in the Holy Land. At this period the Saracens controlled visitors' activities very strictly. Only the Franciscans, based in their House on Mount Syon, were permitted to act as guides to pilgrims who were allowed to stay in the country for a mere 13 days. The sacred sites they were allowed to visit, the routes they followed and the times at which they might visit certain holy places, e.g. the Temple, were rigidly supervised. It is not surprising therefore that most of the sub-headings used by the two pilgrims are identical e.g. "Pilgrimages in Jerusalem", "Pilgrimage in the Vale of Jehoshaphat", "Pilgrimage of Mount Syon", "Pilgrimage of Bethlehem" and "Pilgrimage of Bethany". The feeling of a "package tour" brochure with its list of organised excursions becomes even stronger when each man recounts, on site, not only the canonical episodes from Christ's life and the Gospels which were associated with Bethlehem, the Garden of Gethsamene, Calvary and Emmaus, but also apocryphal anecdotes like the hole in the stone made by Christ when He appeared like a gardener on the first Easter Morning, the well in the Vale of Syloe where the Blessed Virgin washed Christ's baby clothes and the cleft in the rock which opened miraculously to protect the infant John the Baptist. One may assume that these legends were part of the guides' repertoire and the recital of them hardly changed from one year to the next. This is not to deny the religious impact they made on the pilgrims. Both Richard and William adopt the convention of inserting a cross coloured red in their manuscripts beside important locations, whether they are canonical or not. Richard says, "Where ye find the sign of the cross is plenary remission *a poena et culpa* and in other places, where the sign of the cross is not, are 7 years and 7 Lents of Indulgence, and the said Indulgence was granted of Saint Sylvester at the instance of and the prayer of Constantine, the Emperor, and Saint Helena, his mother."

This is almost an exact translation of William Wey's, *Ubi ponitur crux est plena indulgentia a pena et culpa, ubi non ponitur crux sunt indulgentie septem annorum et septem quadragenarum dierum. Predicte indulgentie concesse fuerunt a sancto Silvestro Papa ad preces sancti et magni Constantini imperatoris et sancte Helene matris ejus.* Might these identical quotations originate from a common source, perhaps one supplied by the Franciscans?

This is the most striking similarity between the two narratives. The numerous differences, however, reflect the characters of the two men. William was a priest and a theologian. His quotations from Scripture are more numerous and fuller than those of Richard. He gives details of the hymns the pilgrims sang at important points on their tour and the texts of three sermons which he himself preached in the Temple in 1458 and 1462. He thought more deeply about the places he visited. In 1462 he attempted to find the answers to a number of "Questions", mostly topographical, which could be resolved "on the ground". While Richard is most punctilious in detailing the entrance fees, "tribute", which had to be paid with annoying frequency as the tour progressed – he cites 18 occasions when money must be handed over – William Wey completely ignores this feature of the pilgrimage. Richard does not mention the Franciscans at all, William mentions them frequently. They first appear when the Warden of their House on Mount Syon meets the pilgrims at Rama to welcome them and to celebrate Mass. Subsequently Franciscan Brothers lead them along the *Via Dolorosa*, show them round the Monastery of Mount Syon and spend the night with them shut up in the Church of the Holy Sepulchre. When they went out to Bethlehem William and his party "slept in the Franciscans' cloister", and at the end of their visit they spent their last night in Jerusalem "in the house of Syon".

Another striking difference is the lack of any reference by Richard of Lincoln to the Saracens, until the final page, when he says that on the last lap every man must pay two groats of Venice to the Sultan for safe-conduct. In William's accounts their hostility is ever present. In 1458 they appear as soon as the Venetian galleys arrive in Jaffa harbour, pitching their tents on the sea-shore to ensure that no pilgrims land without permission. After two days' delay, (three days in 1462), confined to their ships, the pilgrims are permitted to land but are then immediately shut up in three caves underground for the night. Here the Saracens count them, a procedure which occurs several times during their stay in the Holy Land. These caves were notorious for filth and lack of amenities, but indulgences could be gained by those who endured the discomfort in the right spirit. Two days later, as the pilgrims journeyed from Rama to Jerusalem, a detachment of Saracen cavalry made a hostile demonstration, but without actually launching an attack on the line of pilgrims who were partly on foot and partly on donkeys. Once in Jerusalem the Saracens refused to allow the pilgrims to enter the Church of the Holy Sepulchre until night-fall and, when they did let them in, they counted them and wrote their names down. The final extortion, as already noted, was on their departure in 1462, when the new lord of Jerusalem demanded another 50 ducats before he allowed the galley to depart for home.

The attitude of the two men towards the Jews is revealing. In his accounts of 1458 and 1462 the only time Wey mentions the Jews is when he repeats the, apocryphal, story of how Jews tried to seize the body of the Blessed Virgin on Mount Syon when the Apostles were taking it out for burial. Richard includes the same legend, but he also has two other stories tending to denigrate the Jews. In the first of these he describes the altar "where the Jews diced for Christ's clothes" and in the second the places "where the Jews constrained Simon to take the cross from Christ". These stories are both told by St Matthew (Chap. 27 vv 27 to 35) and St Mark (Chap. 15 vv 16-24). Both Gospel writers describe those who impressed Simon of Cyrene and later diced for Christ's seamless robe as "soldiers". They would not have been "Jews" and William Wey, who knew the Gospels well, would not have made this error. In perpetuating these items of anti-Semitic propaganda Richard, who was not as familiar with the Bible as William was, was probably repeating misinformation given by the guide.

4. Homeward Bound

One of the psychological features of pilgrimage which still exercises modern pilgrims and those who write about them is the "return", the re-adjustment to "normal" life after the exhilaration, dangers and satisfaction of a successful pilgrimage.

Richard takes his reader from Jaffa to England in eight lines, William (in 1458 and in 1462) in slightly over a page.

Richard mentions two relics on his return journey, the Holy Blood in the church of Sant'Andrea in Mantua and the cheek-bone of St Bernard in the Abbey on the Great St Bernard Pass. Perhaps the medical aspects of these two relics held a special interest for Richard. According to legend the Holy Blood was brought to Mantua by Longinus, the centurion whose spear pierced Christ's side while He was on the Cross. It was shown to the faithful on Ascension Day, and its authenticity was settled by Pope Pius II (Pope from 1458 to 1464), who declared that it had miraculously cured him of gout. The cheek-bone of St Bernard was revered because, according to the legend of the Lactation of the Blessed Virgin Mary, Bernard saw a vision of Our Lady in the Cathedral in Speyer, and, in response to his cry, "*Monstra te, mater*", she expressed milk from one of her breasts which splashed his cheek.

William's concerns were rather more practical. In 1458 he was anxious about possible pursuit by Turkish galleys bent on revenge on Christians in general and the Knights Hospitaller in particular. While he does mention St Dismas (the Good Thief) in Cyprus, St Titus in Crete and the three saints in Jarra, his relief on coming ashore safely at Venice on 6th September, after a voyage of 64 days, is palpable. In 1462 the situation was even more tense. When Wey arrived at Rhodes on 19th August the Grand Master was preparing for a siege and had given orders for a two years' supply of wheat and wine to be collected. The frightening rumours continued. Doubtless the pilgrims on Wey's galley, the *Morosina*, cast frequent glances astern dreading to catch sight of the rise and fall of the oars of a Turkish galley in pursuit. In Cande on 5th September a man told Wey and his companions that the Turk was at sea heading for Rhodes with 300 ships. Again one can feel Wey's relief on landing at Venice on 11th October. In contrast, Richard makes no reference to the threat posed by the Turks to pilgrims at sea.

5. Money, Transport and Accommodation

Both Richard and William were well aware of the cost of a pilgrimage and the necessity of making proper financial provision for it. Richard's account opens with advice to consult the Lombards in London. William's approach is rather different and much more detailed. His first chapter, one of the three written in English, is entitled "Changes of Money from England to Rome and Venice". As one might expect of the man who was repeatedly elected as Bursar by his colleagues, the Fellows of Eton College, he shows great financial acumen. In describing the various currencies which the pilgrim will encounter between Eton and Jaffa, he gives the names of no fewer than 40 types of coin. He also gives advice on where the best exchange rates can be obtained and the pitfalls by which Levantine money-changers will trap the unwary.

Throughout his account Richard gives details of the fees which the pilgrim must pay, e.g. the Channel crossing "from Dover to Calais will cost him two shillings, if he be a footman, and, if he be a horseman, four shillings and three pence." Then there are the river crossings: e.g. "There is a ferry ere we come to Ghent that shall cost a halfpenny for passage" and, "At Bingen there cometh a river (the Nahe) to the Rhine and a ferry over the water, and there a man must pay an obol (a halfpenny) for him and for his horse." Wey does not give this sort of information for the journey to Venice. Once in Venice, however, both men give the cost of a berth on the Jaffa galley as 40 ducats, if meals are taken at the patron's table. Both men quote a price of one and a half ducats for the hire of bedding. (Wey actually gives details of a "sale and return" transaction which comes to the same price as that given by Richard.)

After the departure from Venice, William gives good advice about buying provisions en route, "When you come to a port it is good to be among the first to go ashore for you will thereby purchase what you want at a better price, for example vegetables, chicken, meat, fish, fruit and eggs. Be very careful of the fruit because they very often loosen the bowels and, in those parts, lead to death for Englishmen." There is similar advice later on for the pilgrim after his arrival in the Holy Land, "When you come to get donkeys at Jaffa get there in good time and then you will be able to select a better donkey", and at Rama, "It is a good idea to be among the first to arrive at the place to choose a room and to get fresh water; it will also be sensible to purchase a rush mat from the inn-keeper to put between us and the ground to sleep on, because here are no bed-clothes there." By contrast Richard concentrates on the entry fees which have to be paid at the various sacred sites, e.g. "Ye shall pay at the first entering into the Temple, for your tribute, a Venice groat and a half," and, "In the midst of the Vale of Jehoshaphat is a fair little chapel, in the which is the sepulchre of Our Lady, Saint Mary, and there ye shall pay for your entering three shillings to tribute." In addition to this "tribute" Richard indicates the fees or gratuities which must be paid to the ass-man and the dragoman. Sometimes these payments have a sinister ring, e.g. "Betwixt Ramys ye must have a guide homeward, - two groats of Venice and two shillings. Also to the Sultan for safe conduct, - every man two groats of Venice."

Richard gives the European ferry charges in *obols*, *denarii* and *solidi* (half pennies, pennies and shillings). Other coins which he mentions, for use in the Holy Land, are Venetian *ducats* and *groats*. Venetian coins were readily accepted all over the eastern Mediterranean. After giving the exchange rates for Venetian coins in Corfu, Methoni, Candia, Rhodes and Cyprus, William Wey concludes with the words, "Venetian *ducats*, *groats*, *grossets*, and *soldi* are acceptable in Syria, that is to say in the Holy Land, but no other currency, except at a great disadvantage in the exchange".

The hints dropped by Richard about the mercenary habits of the Sultan are made more explicit by William. In 1462 the pilgrims returned to Jaffa at the end of their 13-day tour in the Holy Land and boarded their galley on 28th July. Wey writes, "We paid the Saracen chiefs 15 ducats for our safe-conduct over this period. A new chief, however, had been sent by the Sultan to govern the city of Jerusalem and my *patronus*, Andreas Morosini, was delayed two days ashore at Jaffa until he paid the new lord of Jerusalem 50 ducats."

Neither Richard nor William says explicitly how they travelled as far as Venice, but there are some clues. Richard mentions ferry charges for horsemen as well as pedestrians and he gives the fees for the hire of donkeys in the Holy Land. One might reasonably assume that he did not travel entirely on foot. Similarly, the speed of William's progress across Northern Europe indicates that he probably rode some of the way, and he too certainly rode a donkey in the Holy Land.

What does appear from both men's accounts is the importance of river transport. Richard and William both made for the Rhine at an early stage in their journeys. Richard used the Rhine and the Swiss and Italian lakes as much as possible. Once over the Alps he headed for the Po, "one of the four rivers of Christendom", and used water transport: "And at the end of Pavia is a fair river ... and the ferry sails to Venice. And four miles from Pavia cometh the river unto the river of Po and from Pavia 40 miles down the river to Piacenza". Richard lists several more places en route, including Cremona, Ostiglia, Lor and finally Chioggia, - "A fair little city and 25 miles to Venice all by water".

The places on the Rhine listed by Richard of Lincoln and William Wey are, on average, about three German miles, i.e. 12 English miles, apart. At this time there were barges on the Rhine which travelled upstream and could have been useful to pilgrims making for Rome or Venice. Medieval illustrations show barges being pulled by teams of men, and sometimes by women, as well as by bullocks. The places in the pilgrims' lists sound like traditional over-night stopping places at the end of a day's towing and suitable accommodation for travellers therefore would be found at them. While pilgrims could and did eat and sleep on the large sea-going galleys between Venice and Jaffa, if they did not put in to a port for one or two nights ashore, they would not, normally, have needed to sleep on the river barges. Wey's list of stage points on the Rhine is to be found in his Chapter 8. A brief extract runs:-

"Andernach; Coblenz 3 miles; Boppard three miles, Bacharach 3 miles, Bingen two miles."

For comparison, Richard's list for the same stretch is:-

"From Andernach three Dutch miles to Coblenz, a fair walled city and a fair river (the Moselle). And over the Rhine is a fair stone bridge. And a mile to Rhens, a little walled town and a castle. And a mile to Saltys, a walled town. And one mile to Boppard, a walled town, and four miles to Bacharach, a walled town, and two miles to Bingen, a walled town, and there cometh a river to the Rhine" (the Nahe).

The present writer has followed Wey's itinerary along this stretch of the Rhine and found that most of the towns mentioned had, in the 15th century, at least one friary, usually a Franciscan one, though there were others as well. Andernach and Coblenz, for example, had Benedictine, Dominican and Franciscan houses, while Boppard had Benedictine, Carmelite and Franciscan (see Brommer and Krummel, *Kloster und Stifte am Mittelrhein*, Koblenz 1998). Similarly almost all the ports which the Venetian galleys visited in Istria, Croatia, Greece, Crete and Cyprus had Franciscan houses. The Milanese, Santo Brasca, writing 30 years later of his pilgrimage in 1480, said, "On the 14th October we entered the port of Lesina (Hvar), a city in Dalmatia, and there we stayed two days waiting for the wind to drop and the sea to calm down a little. As there was no other lodging to be found, the very reverend Misser fratre Pietro da Canedo and I went to lodge at the monastery of the observant friars of the order of St Francis, who received us with such affection, such joy, and such humility as I have no words to describe, and, in spite of their poverty, they did us great honour. I must tell you that in the Levant there is no comfortable lodging to be found, whatever you would be willing to pay for it, except in the monasteries of the observant friars of St Francis." (Newett, *Canon Pietro Casola's Pilgrimage to Jerusalem in the Year 1494*, Manchester 1907, page 397) The Franciscan monastery he describes still stands. When one recalls that the Franciscans, based in their monastery of Mount Syon in Jerusalem, were responsible for providing guides and accommodation for pilgrims throughout their time in the Holy Land, it is not surprising that their hospitality featured so prominently in the earlier stages of the pilgrims' journeys.

6. Conclusion

In their accounts of their journeys Richard of Lincoln and William Wey have left descriptions which, though brief, yet rouse our admiration and stir our imagination. They provoke questions about medieval travel which one would gladly pursue further, but, terse though they are, they still give the reader of today faint echoes of the sounds, sights and smells experienced by two devout and intrepid pilgrims, one a doctor and the other a priest, who crossed Europe to the Holy Land five centuries ago.

APPENDIX

Relics, listed by Richard of Lincoln and William Wey, which were available for pilgrims to venerate.

Part 1. Between England and Venice.

Richard notes:-

Aachen	Our Lady's smock and hair
Cologne	The Kings (i.e. the Magi)
	The 11,000 Virgins (i.e. St Ursula and her companions)
	A nail from Christ's hand
	The body of St Apollonia
	St Peter's staff
	One of the Holy Innocents
Milan	A nail from Christ's hand
Pavia	The body of St Augustine
Venice	The body of St Helena
	The body of St Zacharias
	A bone of St Christopher
	An arm of St George
	The body of St Gregory
	The body of St Theophilus

William lists:-

Aachen	The chemise of the BVM
	One of St Joseph's stockings
Trier	The body of St Matthias
	St Peter's knife which cut off Malchas's ear
	Numerous, unnamed, saints' bodies
St Nicholas in Gaul	An arm of St Nicholas

Venice:

The list in Wey's Chapter 9 begins with St Mark's ring and book and then describes other objects in St Mark's Cathedral, e.g. Moses' stone, St Mark's mosaic of Christ and the phial of blood. Wey continues with a list of more than 50 named saints whose bodies or relics can be seen in the churches of Venice and the islands of the lagoon. This list includes Saints Helena and Zacharias named by Richard. He states, "On Marianus… in St George's church there is St Christopher's leg bone, which is very long". He does not mention by name in this list St George, St Gregory or St Theophilus who appear in Richard's list. He does, however, mention St George in his Chapter 11:- "In St George's Abbey, St George's left arm." In Chapter 8, which refers to the pilgrimage he made in 1458 on the route from Florence south to Rome and then back north to Venice, a route not travelled by Richard, William mentions Spoleto, where "lies Christina", and Assisi, where "lie St Francis and St Clare".

Part 2. Between Venice and Jaffa

Richard's list:-

Rovigno	St Euphemia
Zadar	St Simeon
	St Zoyolus
	St Anastasia
Methoni	St Leo
Rhodes	Thorn from crown of thorns
	Cross made from Maundy Thursday basin
	Hand of St Katherine

William's list:-

Rovigno	St Euphemia (1462)
Zadar	St Simeon (1458 and 1462)

	St Zoyolus (1458)
	St Anastasia (1458)
Dubrovnik	Arm of St Blaise (1458 and 1462)
Corfu	St Arsenius (1462)
Methoni (Axtis)	St Leo (1462)
Rhodes	One of the thorns from Christ's crown (1458 and 1462)
Nicosia	Body of Lord Mountford (1462)
Nicosia (near)	St Mamas (1462)
	Hilarion (1462)

Part 3. On the return journeys

Richard's list:-

| Mantua | The blood of Christ and Longinus's body |
| St Bernard's Abbey | The cheek bone of St Bernard |

William's list:- (all in 1458)

| Salinis (Cyprus) | Cross of the Good Thief (St Dismas) |
| Cande (Crete) | Head of St Titus |

Part 4. Other sites in Wey's Chapter 11

This is a "patchwork quilt" chapter in which Wey has placed a number of pieces of disparate information. It resembles a common-place book and many of the items which appear here are not incorporated in the main narratives of Chapters 7, 9 and 15.

Archipelagus	St George's head
Damascus	St George's column
Rome	In St George's church, the point of the saint's lance
Florence	In Pratus castle, the girdle of the BVM
Constantinople	Stone showing tears of the BVM
Nuremburg	Longinus's spear.

PART 2

The Text

"English 15th-Century medical and astrological compendium"

Reference: MS.8004

Reprinted by kind permission of the Wellcome Library, London

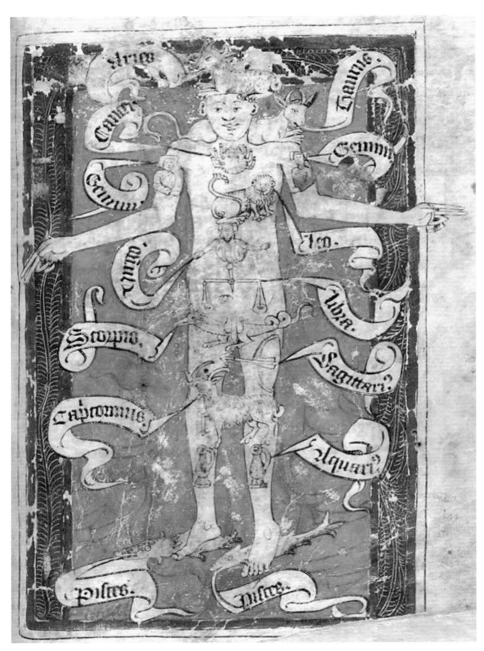

A "zodiac man" featured in the manuscript

75

Who that wyll to Jerusalem gon he muste make
hys chaunge at london w[ith] ye lumbardys And of
yett he make hys chaunge he muste hane a wryte
of chaunge & a wrytt of passage whych ys wryttes
wyll cost hym ij d And / whenne he comyth to donyr
ye wyll bayly wyll hane iij d for bryctynge of y[e] wryt
of passage ye bayze of ye zate wyll hane ij d and
hys fraught. fro donyr to calys wyll coste hym ij s
if he be a fott mane And if he be a horsemane he wyll
hane iij s 4 iiij d And / whenn he comyth to Caleys
ye wyll bayly wott hane iij d & 4 for a horse mane
vij d. ffrome Caleys to granenynge iß m flemysch
myle & a flemysch myle iß in ynglysch myle & yan
he muste pay a peny for hys passage ouy ye watyr
And fome granenyngf iij myle to donbyke a wallyd
towne And fro donbyke v myle to to nedepote A
fay lytyll wallyd towne. And iiij myle to odyngborp
And iij myle to knygges a full fay wallyd towne. 4
iiij myle to opell a vyllage 4 iij myle to grunte
a full full fay wallyd cytte And yer iß a fery of
we come to ganit a yett satt coste a halpeny for p[a]t
ffage And fom ganit to dyndynmont iß 6 myle
and he tlonp yan iß a fery yett satt cost. oß And
6 myle to wnaghtun And iij longe myle to lystot
and n myle to bytte a fayr wallyd towne And iij
myle to byttehutt And he tlonne bytte & bytthntle ay

celo lytyll wallyd tollnys And ho dyffull to maste
ryst is vij myle a fayr wallyd towne ϸ ϸou sall ϸs
passe owϸ a stone brygghe And ϸ passe ϸe brabans ϸ
entyr into lowe allmayne And ho mastrykys iiij duch
mylys to aheyne a full fayr walles tollne And a duch
myle in lawe allmayne is vij ynglyssly mylys And
att aheyne is a fayr pylgrimage to owr lady finote
ϸ to lyr hede of Guy God. And ϸ ay hote bathys
a ϸ is ϸe fyrste tolln of ϸe empatony of almayn
And ho aheyne iiij duch mylys to gulke a lytyll wal
lys tollne ϸ ϸ wyn a wyn afor ϸ zate at gulke
And iiij myle to boyeyne a lytyll wallys tollne ϸ
iiij myle to colapne a full fayr lytte And lowke
beykne ϸ colayne is a lytyll wallys tollne ϸ
a castell And in colayne beyn fay pylgimagis
to ϸe kynghes of colayn And to ϸe xi vyrgyne ϸ
to ϸe poynt of on of ϸe naylys ϸ wass in ϸe
hand of Jhu cryste And to ϸe body of saynte
apollony And to ϸe staffe of saynet per And
to on of ϸe chyps of Jhasll And at colayne
ϸ cometh to ϸe kyne And ϸen up ϸe kyne. iiij
duch myle to bonnen a wallys tollne And iij
duch myle to Remaght iiij duch myle to andy
nake a fayr wallys tollne And ϸer be many
fry castells ϸ tomys enlonge ϸe syd of ϸe
kyne And froms andynake iiij duch myle to

Conclene a fay walled cytte And a fayr Rynez
and ony þe Ryn is a fayr stone brygge And o myle
to Reyns a lytyll walled towne & a castell And o
myle to Saltys a walled towne And on myle to
Bobays a walled towne And iij myle to Baghnagh
a walled towne And too myle to Bynges a wa
lled towne And y cometh a pyver into þe Ryn
& a fery ony þe water & y d mane min sto pay a ob.
for hyme & for hys goyse And fo bynges iij myle
to myens a fayr cytte walled And iij sych myle
to otmeyken a lytyll walled towne iij myle vnto
Wormys a fayr walled cytte And vj myle to Spry
a fayr walled cytte And be tween Wormys and
Spry is a gud Wyrtyngs honse And vij myle to
Lonthyrbmgth a walled towne vij myle to Byssy
oppyl nwele a vylage And iij myle to Strausborgh
a fayr cytte vj myle to maltsyken & myle vnto
otmaken a village iij myle to Basyll a fayr
cytte & þ is a grete brygge ony þe pyver And y
nwsse þe genall somsell of all cleygy of cysty
ndome. And fo Basyll iij myle to thynsse a
lytyll village walled towne a full ill waye
And att thynsse is a fayr Ryner & a fay brygge
ony þe Ryn And fo Basyll to amane passe
þe mowntayne a sych myle is vj pyghyshy
myle And fo Thynsse iij myle to Snymaye

A lytyll wallyd towne And ij longe myle to lucca a fay
fcytyll wallyd towne And þ is a fayr byngfe of þoo and
a longe And it is lytlyd w' tyle & is in þat byoo
& it is halfe a myle longe And it is on þe fayryst
wor of all þe waylo And þ is mych fyfch in þ myne
And on þe conth syd of þe towne þ is a mowntayn
And in þe toppe of þe mowntayn þ is a gret ftandyng
wat' in þe whych we hop say þe body of goylat is
boyyd And paw day nott litt no ymgs come þ yno
w olwtyn ordynanics of mono of þe towne is þe
And for if any ymgs be cafte in þe sayd ftandyngs
wat' þ wnlt yyfe fuch atompofts & ftoyyyn' þat þe
pepule aryst to pichs in þe cntrey And halucon
paw mofts to tuke soys fayy for þe wat is my ouch
myle longs to flowlyngs a lytytt village And þer
is now ody way bott ony þe watt And fro fferet
yngs ij ouch myle to waffhyn a lytyll village &
yen cntyr so to monte Godayd And fro waffhyn ij
myle to þe hospitale of capnt Godayd And fro þe
hofpitall ij myle to þe toppe of þe monte Godayd &
ij myle downe þe banks a fnlt ret way to Gyott a lytytt
village And fro gyott ix lumbayd myle to feyte
a lytytt village & ij lumbayd myle math ij puglyfh
myle And be noth gyott & feyt is a monte y whych
is callyd monte tyayyo or ctt emonto And fro feyt
xx lumbayd myle to Bylyfon a fayy wallyd town

And þat is þe furste loke of lumbardy & xij myle vnto
Brygon lugann And it is amonte be Hene Belyson
& Brygon lugann whych is callyd monte Syndy
And att þe brygth lugann is a fayr wat' whypche is
callyd þe wat' of lugann & it is vij myle longe &
þ myste to feyr ony And it is a lytyll village at þe
este end of þe wat'. And fro þe wat' xij myle vnto
Somys a fayr wallyd towno And it is a fayr wat'
And xvj myle to Caffandmatu a village And vj
myle to mylayn a fayr wallyd towno And þer is of
þe naylis þ wer in þe hande of cryste And it is vnd
a hygh gate & ʋ lawmpis brymynge dayly aboute itt.
And fro mylano xx myle to palwe a fayr wallyd
towno & an vmufite goldyn And be Hene a myle
& palwe þ is a fayr payke wel wallyd v5 tyle And
þ in beyne lybeyds & lyone & all mair of odyr dor
And maynolwffe man of foldys And a full ſtronge
castell And in palwe is a fayr pylgimage to þe
body of Sayut Auſtin. þe holy Soctor Jn þe same
chych is a well þat twelych of Sʋiſs cshiosſe both
þe mane & þe womene if þai dynke of þat watyr
And at þe ond of palwe is a fayr jynoy And aftone
brygth ony þe jyn towayd Jeno And þ fayr folke vnto
wonyſs be wat' And vij myle fro palwe cometh
jynoy vnto þe jyn of þoo And fro palwe xl myle
Sawno þe jyney to plefannte is a fayr wallyd cytte

And y' bou y castelle m' þe Cytte And þe tbone yanke
e plesaunce is, a lytel Wallyd towne Whych is cald
Ajend xiiij myle fro[m]e g[r]awe z fro plesaunce xxx
dawne þe jnd to Gjemow a fayr Wallyd towne And
xxxij myle to Bnsholl a lytylt village And bothe
Gemon z Bnssolt beyn ij lytell Wallyd townys y
Roeland was capptayn ac men cayn z y be many
townys and castelle endlonge þe Rynys of þo for
it is out of þe my Rynys of cristyndome And fro
Bnssolt xxvi myle to Bngo forþ a full fayr village
z a castell. And fro Bnygo xij myle to hostilia A
fayr lytylt towne z a fayr castell And xvij myle
to Stalett a fayr vyllage And xxbij to Cosbula
a litilt village. And xvij myle to Loy a fayr lytylt
village And xviij myle to Clege a fay lytte cytte
And xxb myle to venyse aff be watt a full fayr
cytte z it standyth aff in þe ecé And y is a fayr
pylgrimage to þe body of sayncte elhjn And to
Saucte zachans he fad of Sarut Johan Bayntiste
And þe bone of saucte Cristofor And ou of þe
nynte of Saucty George And y lyth in þe toltme
of saucty zachans þe body of sauct Gregory y
doctny And þe body of saucty Theophils And
in þe mynntrý of þe Cytte Which is of sancte
mayke y is a gret aff of jed mayn be y which
yat z jate Ricolys iten Whew he y þed vnto y
fassyllt of hendns. At venyse a mans mnste tak

hys sale And a mane muste pay for hys passage
w'in ye vale as ye patrons & he may acord And p
moste y any mane pay as xvj or lx ducatt & to be
att ye patrons bord & ye bedd will coste p an
ducatt & a haufe And frome venyse .l. myle to
Renens a fayr lytyll wallyd towne & a mynstry
& y lyth ye body of saynete Onsenyus And fro
Renens xx myle to polo an oldj wallyd towne
& a full fay hanyn & y is an old place whych
is callyd Rowland place & y ben many towmb
of stone in ye fold abowte ye towne & on y
corth syde of ye towne y is a town whych is
callyd Rowlandstowp And fro polo .l.l. myle
payp a fayr lytyll wallyd towne And pey is
a fayr pylgymage to ye body of sanete Edmond
And att ye mynst of sanct Berthalme is a fayr
pylgymage of sanct Anastasij whych wasse att
ye byrth of our lord Jesu Crist And fro payp .c.
myle to z.l. myle to Crysfull a lytyll wallyd
towne And a hundyrth myle to dyogose a fayr
lytyll wallyd towne & a parch And .l. myl & xl.
to Dyrasse a wallyd towne And Ct yl myle to
Dyrfelles a fay lytyll towne & a castell & y is
be twene Dyrasse & Crysselles a chapoll whych
is callyd Godspa And y se sall hey a myracle
for y is a lytyll lawmpe whych brynyth boye
nyzte & day And it is bott one flode in y sey

and a fayr pylgrimage to our lady sancte mary. And home page
to godyne ccc myle a fayr hanyne and a wallyd towne and
yer is a fayr pilgimage on the corye a myle fro the towne
to the body of Sanct leo the holy hermytte And fro godon
ccc myle to candy a fayr wallyd towne a fayr hanene
And ccc myle to Rodys a full fayr wallyd towne And
a fayr castell & y ben fayr pylgrimags to a poynt of y
towne of Jhu cryste y he was crownyd wt in tyme of
passion And it byngpone ony gud fryday as pat sayn
in the tym of hys passion And on of the penysse y
cryste wasse sold for And to a gosse y wasse made
of the basyn y cryste wasthyd hys dysyples fete p
on shyr thursday And to the hand of Sanct katne &
fro Rodys one myle to joyte jasse & the apt y m the
holy land And m the ccc a myle of the corvth sto
from jasse y is a stone y saynte pot stod on also
he sthyd & y apoyd cryste vnto hyme And att
jasse a mane sall pay the patho a Ducatt or he passe
the gate and when he comyth to lond he muste
pay for hys trubute En Ducatt & en venysse gth
& y a mane muste take hys asse And fro jasse x
myle Ramus a fayr towne and he muste pay a
gte to hys ass mane And fro Ramus to the cytte of
lydde jn the whych saynct George wasse martyd
& y a mane muste pay a Ducatte & vj groth to
the gte drogemane for sakynesse of the way be
we thone Ramus & and jerusalem. Drogemane for

cobynesse of þe way be twene Rame & Jerm is betwe
grete & in Rames was Ioseph born þt tuke crist of þe cro
And schall vndyrstand þt yf þe 3e finds þe chirche of þe crosse
is plen remyssion a pena & culpa & in oþer place þe
chirche of þe crosse is no3te & vij 3er and lx lentius of
indulgence & þe sayd indulgence was grantid of
sein Syluestre at þe instaunce of & þe prior of Constan̄
þe emperour & saynct Anne hys moder Also in Rames
is a chyrch & a sepulcre of saynct Bennett þe prophet &
fro Rames xij myle to þe Castell of Emaus in þe which
castell is a chyrch wher in dyscyple knewe crist in brekyng
of breed aftyr hys resurreccion Also þr is a chyrch on þe
left hand, two myle fro Emaus in þe which is þe
body of Sanct marie Cleophe on of þe xij dysciple
And fro þe sepulcre of Cleophe vij myle to þe cite
of Ierusalom. Pylgrimagis of þe . . . cite of Jerm

Thyes bene þe pylgrimagis of þe cite of Jerm
þe fyrste is be for þe temple Dor þt is a in
fynar stone of whyte alybaunstyr þt crist reste hym
selfe on hys crosse when he wente toward þe mounte
of caluary Also þr is a temple in Ierm þe whiche is
callyd cristus temple & is fast nay at þe fyrste entryng
into þe temple for 3our tribute a venysse grote & iii
hawse And at þe second entrynge iiij grot litle at þe
iij entrynge ij venysse grot of 3e passe þe pylgrimage
in to þe temple ffyrste þt is on þe south syd of þe
temple a chapell þt crist apeyryd fyrste to hys mod'

80

demacon of mane kynd. And þ is a mortasse in þe chyrche
of þe place whych was whene cryste yeldyd goste.
✠ A pena &c Also afore agayne þe chapell þer is a
place abit wer a sepulcry wher cryste laye whene
he was takyne of þe crosse & anoyntyd & laid i a clothe.
✠ A pena &c Also in þe weste end of þe temple is a
lytell chapell in þe whych is a fayre shappyd stone þ
þe angell satt & sayd to þe iij maijs wchome sek jee
And þai sayd jesus of nazareth. And þe angell said
he is rysyne & gone. Also in anodyr chapell wt in þe
chapell is þe sepulcry of our lady jesus cryste
Also in myddys of þe quier in þe temple is a hole
in a stone þ cryste sayd to hys dyscyplis her is þe
myddys of þe wayld. Also þe is a chapell þ þe sepulcre
of adam is. Also on þe ryjte hand as je go vnto þe
temple wayd is a chapell þ our lady a sayrit jon stod
whan cryste sayd vnto hys modyr woman se þi
sone. And on þe same syde is a chapll of saincti jon
baptyste. Also on þe left hand þe temple dor
is a fayr chapell of mary mawdleyne. Also þ be þe
stacions abonte þe temple in þe cytte of jerusale
þe fyrste is whey þe jewis conßreyud Symon to
take þe crosse att jesu whene he wente to þe
mownts of calvarie. Also þer is a place þ jesus and
pylatte sate whene pilat clethe cryste of hys clothe
cypud & of þe pictyvngit A pena &c Also a lytytll þer
is þe howse wher our lady lyned, a stole. Also on
þe

left hand a lityll pons is ye place of herodys & yody was
cryste ledd a for herod ✠ Also a lytytt pons is prelett/
howse in ye whyche cryste was / borowden to ye polyp
And / somgodd/ Also on ye ryzte hand is ye temple of
Salamon in ye whyche our lady carnet mary was
weddid ✠ Also a lyrett pons is ye howse of joachym
& Anne hys wysse whor our lady was borne ✠ Also
a lyrott pons is a lytytt wettyr whyche is callyd
probatica piscina in ye whyche many lepyrs is holyd/
be ye vertu of a tre of ye holy crosse yt lay jnn many
zerys/ Also a lytytt fromo ye temple of Salamon is
porta aurea be ye whyche cryste entyrd/ into ye cytte of
jralme Croudur syttynge apon an Asse/ Also ✠ Also a lytytt
pons is a zate be ye whyche Saint Stebyn ledd
owte of ye cytte whan he was stonyd/ to ded/
⊓ lytytt w owte ye Cytte halp of ye vale of josaphat
yer is a place yer Saint Stebyn wasse stonyd/to ded/
Also a lytytt pons in mydd ye vale of josaphat is/
tomston redyon alwey a tre of ye holy crosse lay for a
brygge many zers And/ aftyrward/ was/ caste into ye
patica piscina Also in ye mydd ye vale of josaphat
is afar lytel chapell in ye whyche ys/ ye sepulc
of our lady Saint mary dessendynge xlvii greeis
& yt ye sall pay for zour entryng in · iiij d to tbute
✠ Also a lytott pons is a place whor cryste preyd/
to ye fadyr of heuyne ⸳
⊓ joius yer place a lytytt is/ a gardyne us ye

81

Whyche cryste was/ takyne of þe iewys/ as þat iudas
had be trayd/ hyme Also a lytyll vp hyer in þe way
to wayd/ mownte olyvete is a place wher cryste sayd/
to hys dyscyples wakyn & pry þat ze entryngete in to
temptacion Also a lytel pece is a stone þ sancte thomas
resayvd/ þe gyrdyll of oure lady whos sche flyed/ vnto
hevyn Also a lytyll pece in þe same way is a
place þ cryste wepyt/ apon þe cyte of ierusalem.
Sayinge þ þat nott be on stone lefte vp on oþyr. Also a
lytel pece is/ a place wher þe angel apeyyd/ to oure
lady w þe palme Sayinge suche a day þ salt be takyn
into hevyn. Also a lytel pece is an hyll whyche is/
clepyd galilee þ cryste apeyyd/ to hys/ apostylle aftyr
hys resurrexion. Also þ is a place wher þe chyldren of
israel dyd/ worsshype to cryste whan þai caste branches
of olyve trees in hys/ way. Also apon mownte olyvete
is/ a olde/ temple þ cryste ascend into hevyn & þer
is sene þe steppys/ in þe ston And/ at mownt olyvete
a mane myste pay a d for hys/ trybute. Also a
lytyll pece is þe sepulcre of polago Also moste
dynge downe þe banke is an olde/ chyrch þer þ apostle
mad/ þe crede/. Also in þe same way þ is a place þer
cryste prayd/ ofttyme to hys/ apostles. Also in þe same
way is a place wher cryste taught þe apostylle þe pater
noster Also a lytel pece is a place þ oure lady restyd
eny day vysytynge þe holy placys of þe walle of
Syloe. Also a lytel pece by þe way þer is a place

Wher Sancte James þe lesse was þe tyme of þe passion
& to crste was þysshue fro deth to lyfe. Also abowne in
þe same place is þe sepule of zacharie þ justys
Also in þe vale of Syloe is a wole þ our lady wasshd
þe clopes of our lord Jhu crste in his childhod. Also
Alytyll hens on þe ryȝte hand is a place whych is
zatatond Syloe wher crste gafe syȝte to þe blynd man
Also alytyll hens is a place ysaias þe pphett was
sawne wt a two sawe in Sundy. Also alytyll hens
a places lyke caues in þe gurche þe Appostyls was
hyd in þe tyme of þe passion of Jhu crste Also
alytyll hens is a place þat is callyd Acheldemaci þ
was bonȝte for xxxti penys þ crste was sold for se
þ here all crsten pylgyns herbuyes pylgimage of mot sponn

A lytel from mownte Syon is a place þ þe Juys
wold haue a refrd our lady when þe Apls
bary hir to be buryet. Also a lytylt hens is a place
wher Sanct Steuyn þe s tyme was buryet Also att
þe est end of þe gurche at mont Syon þ þe holy
lame was fostrd. Also att þe noȝth Syde of þe
gurche is a stone þ crste stod apon when he
pchyrd to his dyssypuls. Also þ is anoþ ston þ
our lady satte apon in þe tyme of þchynge of
crste. Also a lytylt hens is a place þ our lady pyd
þe space of iiij ȝer aftyr þe passion of crste
Also þ is a place þ our lady dyed Also a lytill
hens is a place þ sancte Jon þe Euugelyste sayd

masse to owr lady sancta maria. Also at ye hye awter in
ye chyrch of mownte syon is a place yat cryste made hys
mawndy wt his apostyles + Also on ye ryʒte hand of ye
awter is a place yat cryste wasschyd hys apostyllis feete
apone sheyr thursday. Also wtoute ye chyrch on ye south
syde is a chapell A pone A vaute yat ye holy goste dyssendyd
on wytsonday + Also in ye cloystr is a lytyll chapell yat
sancte Thomas of ynde putt his hand to cryste wowndys
+ Also in ye north syde a lytyll frome mownte syon is a
place yhere cayphas howsse was in ye whyche cryste
was in prisone. & yat is ye stone yt was putt on ye sep
ulcyr of cryste for sekyrnesse yt he schuldy noʒte ryse, whyche
place is kept wyrsschypffully wt gloty. Also a lytill fro
ydat place yat sancte James ye moy masse hody & tuke hte
ett to sprayne thronze ye myzte of Jhu cryste. Also on
ye lefte hand, ys a chapell of sancte Damd. Also it is
fro Jerln on myle to bedlem pylgrmage of Bedlem

Eyr manie misse pray it ye cryynge in to yt chapill
temple A worsschyp grote foy his typbwte + A noe
to his dssmans. Also in mydys ye qnoy of ye temple is
a chapell as it woy A furse whdnoth ye ryyty yat jhu
cryste was boyne + Also in ye same chapell cryste was
layd he theyr a noy + A nasse. Also in ye syys ony ye
ryʒte hand, is an awtyr yat ye thye kynges of colayne
mayd yat offeryngs. Also in ye cloystr of ye same tem
ple is a chapell whsshondyngs wndnoth ye oryty yat
is ye stody + ye stole of sancte Jerome & yat tryyysylys

pe hyllys ho chyldryn into Egypte Also a lytill pond ys pe
semple of pe chyld of Israel. Also it is vij myle fro pe
Bedlem to moonte jude. Also in pe moonte jude is a
chapell in pe whych sanct Jon Baptiste was bore
+ per is pe cryste y oppynd by pe selfe p he was hyd in
+ per pays a mane to tribute a venyss grote. Also a lyt
pond is a place y our lady + sanct Elyzab mett. yyy
peres hyrte + in p place made our lady pe psalme
magnificat. Also a lytill pond is a fayr well wher
Elyzab waschyd sanct Jon clepis in hylly hed. Also
half a myle pond p is a chapy p sancte Jon Baptiste
was borne. Also iij myle frome moonte jude to
ward Jerusalem is a chyrch p a tre of pe holy grosse
growey + ho pond to Jorten ij myle + y zony Assman
will hane a venyss grote. Hilly mylg of Bet any

ius pe est party. ij myle ho plue toward Jurydon
in betony is a temple p sayncte lazar was byryet
in pe same temple is a lytill chapell p cryste stod
when he raysyd pe lazar to deth to lyfe. + for otringe
ho sull pay iij d to tribute + Also in betony is pe house
of Symon pe lepyr in pe whych cryste foy gasse mary
maudlayn h sind. Also it pe opte end of betony p
cryste raysyd hymis to his Apostylt when marytha sayd
unto hymis. Lord had p born hey lazar my brod had
nought born ded. Also a lytill pond is pe house of
marytha in pe whych cryste raysyd hymis of tymp. Also
Also a lytill pond is pe house of mary maudlayn
To moonte tayyyn yyy myle.

fro Betony in þe whych is a chapell þ crist fastid xl dayes
& þ a mane payd to typhnte a soliðs Also in þe tope
of þe same mownte is a place þ þe devils sett crist
& shewyd hyme all þe rychesse of þe worlds & sayd
if þ will fall dokne & worshype me þ sall have
all þes rychesse. Also. ij. myle þens is þ cytte of
Jericho in þe whych crist oft tymes. Also fro Jericho
is ij myle & a hase to þe chapell of sanct Johne
Baptiste. Hase a myle fro flumyoþdayn in þe whych
sanct Jon Baptyste crist. Also flumyoþdayn rynys
weste in to þe may morte & it is a fayr ryner. And
it is allway mody as it wer tymbyld. Be þe whyche
may morte. Sodom & gomorr wer smyttne & dystryed
Also at Jorsln a mane þ will to flumyoðayne rynste
pay yn venysse groth for his tribute & at flumyoþdayn
iij d for his dyore mane. Also be Abyss Lamps þe
rynste have a grote gome wayd ij grote of venysse & ij solið
Also to þe soldane for a sabe cmidyth. eny mane ij grot
of venysse. Also to zour asmitan eny all cyrtasy cin man
so venysse groth. Also home Lamps to passe home wayd
to zour asmano eny mane as þer may acord for sum
iij venysse grote & dn this. Also in þe way home in
Cumbordy. is a cytte þe whyche is callyd mantway &
þ is of þe blody of Jhon criste. Whych iþ logi gonzte
þody yw þe þe sper & þor hys longes bodely in hys sep
nle. Also in þe mownte. Bayned, in a Abbay is a

theme of ꝑ... And ꝑ cheke bone of ... ...
... come we homeward through ...
... of ...

... of ...

Hor helth of body con for cold ꝑ ...
... no iulle mete take and body ꝑ to
... helsom wyne feed ꝑ on lyte bred
w... abbyt... ꝑf wp ho ꝑt mote less
w... womene land hime no... flesshly to do
wp... ꝑ slepe dyuke no... on ꝑt cop...
... toward bed a it morne boy... to
... ma... lttle fyte sore
And if it be so ꝑt locchid do fyle
ꝑon take and bed to pmgf th...
Tempat ꝺyete t rompit t... ...
... malia... for now... now...
... in tro... glad in ...
Euy w lytill content w suffic...
... gochynge bott on lyte ꝑt day...
If hele take make ꝑd ꝑ...
To any tale done gyfe ꝑt no ...
Be nott to hasty nor sotganly veng...
Surtas of langage of fedynge mesurabyll
Of sundry moth non... gloth at ꝑ table.
In fedynge ientyll ꝑindent in dalyannce
Close of tonge of wordys dysshavabyll

PART 3 - Translation of the Text

Anyone wishing to go to Jerusalem must change his money in London with the Lombards.[1] Before he does this he must have a writ of exchange and a writ of passage. These two writs will cost him two shillings. When he comes to Dover the water bailiff will take four pence for the writ of passage while the bailiff of the gate will have two pence and his freight-charge. Dover to Calais will cost him two shillings, if he is on foot, but if he is a horseman he will pay four shillings and three pence.[2] When he reaches Calais the water bailiff will have three pence. It is six pence for a horseman. It is three Flemish miles from Calais to Gravelines; a Flemish mile is three English miles. There he must pay a penny to cross the water. From Gravelines it is three miles to Dunkirk, a walled town, and five miles from Dunkirk to Newport, a fair little walled town. Then it is four miles to Ostend [Odyngborghe], three miles to Bruges, a full fair walled town, four miles to Aalter, a village, and four miles to Ghent, a full fair walled city. Before he comes to Ghent there is a ferry which will cost a halfpenny for the passage. It is five miles from Ghent to Dendermonde and between them is a ferry that will cost one obol [a halfpenny]. Next, five miles to Mechelen, four long miles to Aarschot, two miles to Diest, a fair walled town, and three miles to Hasselt. Between Diest and Hasselt are two little walled towns. It is four miles from Hasselt to Maastricht, a fair walled town, where you will cross a stone bridge to leave Brabant and enter Lower Germany.

From Maastricht it is four Dutch miles to Aachen, a full fair walled town. A Dutch mile in Lower Germany is four English miles. At Aachen there is a fair pilgrimage to Our Lady's smock and hair. There too there are hot baths. It is the first town of the Emperor of Germany.[3] From Aachen four Dutch miles bring you to Julich, a little walled town where a river runs in front of the town-gate.[4] Then it is three miles to Bergheim, a little walled town, and three miles to Cologne, a full fair city. Between Bergheim and Cologne there is a little walled town and a castle. In Cologne the pilgrim can revere the Kings of Cologne, the 11,000 Virgins, the point of one of the nails that penetrated the hand of Jesus Christ, the body of Saint Apollonia, the staff of Saint Peter and one of the children of Israel.[5] One reaches the Rhine at Cologne. Next, four Dutch miles up the Rhine, is Bonn, a walled town. After that it is three Dutch miles to Remagen and three Dutch miles to Andernach, a fair walled town. There are many fair castles and towns along the side of the Rhine. Three Dutch miles from Andernach is Coblenz, a fair walled city, and a fair river [the Moselle].[6] There is a fair stone bridge over the Rhine. A mile further on is Rhense, a little walled town with a castle, and after another mile Saltys, a walled town. Next it is one mile to Boppard, a walled town, and four miles to Bacharach, a walled town, and two miles to Bingen, a walled town, where a river [the Nahe] flows into the Rhine. Here one takes a ferry over the water, which will cost a man an obol for himself and his horse.[7] From Bingen it is four Dutch miles to Mainz, a fair walled city, three Dutch miles to Oppenheim, a little walled town, four miles to Worms, a fair walled city, and six miles to Speyer, another fair walled city. There is a good rest-house between Worms and Speyer.[8]

It is seven miles to Lauterbourg, a walled town, another seven miles to the village of Bischwiller, then three miles to Strasburg, a fair city, six miles to Marckolsheim, five miles to the village of Ottmarsheim and three miles to Basel. This is a fair city with a great bridge over the river. The General Council of all the clergy of Christendom was held here.[9] From Basel it is four miles to Thrusse, a little walled town, and a very poor road it is. At Thrusse there is a fair river with a fair bridge over the Rhine.[10] After Basel one has to cross the mountains. A Dutch mile is six English miles. After Thrusse it is three miles to Sursee, a little walled town,[11] and two long miles to Lucerne, a fair little walled town. Here there is a fair long wooden bridge which is roofed with tiles. It is eight paces broad and half a mile long. It crosses the fairest river in the world which abounds in fish.[12] On the south side of the town there is a mountain on the top of which is a large expanse of still water in which, so runs the story, Pilate's body is buried. You must not dare to let anything fall into it without the permission of the town council. If anything is thrown into the said water such a great tempest and storm will arise that the people in the neighbourhood are likely to perish.[13] After Lucerne you must take the ferry to the small village of Flüelen because the lake is four Dutch miles long and there is no other way except by water.[14] From Flüelen it is three Dutch miles to Wassen, a little village at the approach to Mount Gotthard.[15] From Wassen it is two miles to the hospital of Saint Gotthard and two more miles from the hospital to the top of the Mount Gotthard. It is then two miles down the slope, by a really poor road, to Göschenen, a small village. From Göschenen it is ten Lombardy miles to Faido, a small village.[16] Three Lombardy miles make two English miles. Between Göschenen and Faido is a mountain which is called Monte Trappe or Ettemonte. After Faido it is twenty Lombardy miles to Bellinzona, a fair walled town.[17]

This is the first sight of Lombardy. It is then twelve miles to Lugano. Between Bellinzona and Lugano there is a mountain called Monte Cenere.[18] At Lugano is a fair lake called Lake Lugano. This is eight miles long and you must take a ferry to cross it to a small village at the east end of the lake.[19] It is twelve miles from the lake to Como, a fair walled town where too there is a fair lake. After sixteen miles you come to the village of Cassanamata. Eleven miles further on is Milan, a fair walled town. Here there is one of the nails which pierced the hand of Christ; it is under a high gate and has five lamps burning about it daily.[20] Next, twenty miles from Milan, comes Pavia, a fair walled town, which has a university.[21] Between Milan and Pavia there is a fair park, with a good tiled wall. It contains leopards, lions and all kinds of deer together with an amazing variety of birds.[22] There is also a very strong castle. In Pavia the pilgrim sites include the body of the holy doctor, Saint Augustine. In the same church there is a well which heals various ailments, both those of men and those of women, if they drink its water.[23] At the far side of Pavia is a fair river which is crossed by a stone bridge carrying the road to Genoa. The ferry sails along the river to Venice. Four miles from Pavia the river [*Ticino*] enters the river Po.[24] It is forty miles down the river from Pavia to Piacenza, a fair walled city where there are two castles. Between Pavia and Piacenza, fourteen miles from Pavia, is a little walled town called Arena. Cremona, a fair walled town, is thirty miles down river from Piacenza. It is then thirty-two miles to Brescello, a small village. Between Cremona and Brescello are two little walled towns. People claim that Roland was the captain there.[25] There are many towns and castles along the river Po which is one of the four Rivers of Christendom. Twenty-five miles from Brescello is Burgoforte, a full fair village with a castle. After Burgoforte it is twelve miles to Ostiglia, a fair little town, which also has a fair castle, seventeen to Stellata, a fair village, twenty-seven to Corbola, a small village, twenty-two to Loreo, a fair little village, and eighteen to Chioggia, a fair little city. From here it is twenty-five miles, all by water, to Venice, a full fair city, which is entirely surrounded by the sea. The important relics here are the body of Saint Helena, Saint Zacharias, the father of Saint John Baptist, a bone of Saint Christopher and one of the arms of Saint George. In the tomb of Saint Zacharias lie the bodies of Saint Gregory, the Doctor, and Saint Theophilus. In the city's cathedral, which is dedicated to Saint Mark, is the great red marble stone upon which Christ knelt when He prayed to His heavenly Father.[26]

At Venice a man must board his galley. He should agree the fare for the voyage with the patron of the galley. The most that anyone should pay for his passage is sixteen ducats, or forty if he takes his meals at the patron's table. A bed will cost you another ducat and a half.[27] From Venice it is one hundred miles to Rovinj, a fair little walled town with a cathedral where lies the body of Saint Euphemia.[28] Twenty miles from Rovinj is Pula, an old walled town with a full fair harbour. Here there is an old palace called Roland's Palace; there are also many stone tombs in the fields around the town. On the south side of this town is a tower known as Roland's Tower.[29] From Pula you sail one hundred and fifty miles to Zadar, a fair little walled town, where one can make a fair pilgrimage to the body of Saint Simeon. In the cathedral of Saint Zoyolus the pilgrim can see the relic of Saint Anastasia who attended the birth of Our Lord Jesus Christ.[30] It is one hundred miles from Zadar to (*gap*) and another fifty miles to Korçula, a little walled town.[31] One hundred miles further on is Ragusa [*Dubrovnik*], a fair little walled town, and a rich one it is too.[32] From here it is one hundred and forty miles to Durres, a walled town, and another one hundred and forty miles to Corfu, a fair little town with a castle. Between Durres and Corfu is a chapel called Cassiopi, where you will hear about a miracle. In this chapel is a small lamp which burns night and day although it is only filled once a year. There is also a pilgrim site commemorating Our Lady, Saint Mary.[33] From there it is three hundred miles to Methoni, a walled town with a good harbour. Here one can perform a fair pilgrimage, by going a mile south of the town, to the body of Saint Leo, the holy hermit.[34] Next, three hundred miles from Methoni, one comes to Candia [*Herakleion*], a fair walled town with a good harbour.[35] Another three hundred miles bring you to Rhodes, a full fair walled town with a fair castle. Here the pilgrim can see a thorn from Jesus' crown with which He was crowned at the time of His Passion. This is said to flower only on Good Friday in Passiontide. Also on display is one of the pennies that Christ was sold for, and a cross made from the basin that Christ used when He washed His disciples' feet on Shyr [*Maundy*] Thursday. There is also the hand of Saint Katherine.[36] From Rhodes it is seven hundred miles to the port of Jaffa where one enters the Holy Land.[37]

In the sea a mile south from Jaffa is the stone on which Saint Peter stood when he was fishing and Christ appeared to him.[38] At Jaffa you must pay the patron a ducat before you can pass the gate. When you disembark you must pay the fee of seven ducats and seventeen Venetian groats. This is where you must hire a donkey. From Jaffa it is ten miles to Rama, a fair town where you must pay the donkey-man a groat.[39] From Rama to the city of Lydda, where Saint George was martyred, will cost you a ducat and six groats.[40] The fee to the dragoman for a safe-passage between Rama and Jerusalem is nine Venetian groats. Rama was the birthplace of the Joseph who took Christ off the Cross.[41] I should explain that at the places where you see the sign of the cross you can obtain plenary remission *a poena et culpa* [from punishment and guilt]. In other places, where there is no sign of the cross, you may receive seven years and seven Lents of Indulgence. These Indulgences were granted by Saint Sylvester at the instance of and at the prayer of Constantine, the Emperor, and Saint Helena, his mother.[42] In Rama too is a church with a sepulchre of the prophet Saint Samuel.[43] From Rama it is twelve miles to the castle of Emmaus, which contains a church where two disciples recognised Christ in the breaking of bread after His Resurrection. Two miles from Emmaus, on the left, is the church which contains the body of Saint Mary Cleophas, one of the twelve disciples.[44] From here it is seven miles to the city of Jerusalem.

Pilgrimages in the city of Jerusalem

These are the pilgrimage sites in the city of Jerusalem. The first is in front of the temple door where there is a square stone of white alabaster on which Christ rested with His cross when He was on the way to Mount Calvary. In Jerusalem there is a temple which is called Christ's Temple where on your first visit you must pay a fee of one and a half Venetian groats.[45] A second visit costs four groats and a third two Venetian groats. The payment must be made before you enter the temple. The first thing you see is on the south side of the temple. This is the chapel where Christ appeared first to His Mother after His Resurrection and said "*Salve, sancta parens*" ["Hail, Holy Mother"]. To the right of the altar is a window where stands a pillar to which Christ was bound and beaten with scourges in Pilate's house. In the same window is a little pillar to which Christ was bound in Caiaphas's house.[46] *A poena et c.***+**. On the left of the altar stands a small cross made from the Holy Cross. In the middle of the chapel is a round stone of various colours where Saint Helena verified the cross upon which Christ died by raising a dead man to life.[47] In front of the same chapel door there is a round stone with a hole in the middle where Christ appeared to Mary Magdalene after His Resurrection in the form of a gardener and said "*Noli me tangere*" ["Touch me not"].[48] **+** *A poena et c*. On the same side of the temple there is a chapel where Jesus Christ was imprisoned while the nails and the cross were being prepared. There is also an altar where the Jews diced for Christ's clothes.[49]

At the east end of the temple you go down thirty-two steps to a chapel where, inspired by the Holy Ghost, Saint Helena found the cross.[50] **+** *A poena et culpa.* A little above this is a chapel founded for the worship of Saint Helena. A little further in the same chapel is a pillar where Jesus Christ was spat upon and crowned with thorns.[51] Further on again, up nineteen steps, is a chapel which is Mount Calvary where Christ suffered His Passion for the redemption of mankind. Here is a crack in the rock face which split when Christ gave up the ghost.[52]**+** *A poena et c.* In front of the chapel door is the place, a sort of sepulchre, where Christ lay when He was taken from the cross, anointed and wrapped in a cloth. **+** *A poena et c*. At the west end of the temple is a little chapel in which is a square stone where the angel sat and said to the three Marys, "Whom seek ye?"[53] They replied, "Jesus of Nazareth". Then the angel said, "He is risen and gone". In another chapel within the chapel is the sepulchre of Our Lord Jesus Christ. In the middle of the corner in the temple is a stone with a hole where Christ said to His disciples, "Here is the centre of the world".[54] There is also a chapel with the sepulchre of Adam.[55] As you enter the temple precinct there is a chapel on the right in the place where Our Lady and Saint John stood when Christ said to His Mother, "Woman see your son".[56] The chapel of Saint John Baptist is on the same side. To the left of the temple door is a fair chapel of Mary Magdalene.

Then there are the Stations outside the Temple in the city of Jerusalem. The first is where the Jews made Simon take the cross from Jesus, when He was on the way to Mount Calvary.[57] There too is the place where Jesus and Pilate sat when Pilate asked Christ about His Disciples and their preaching. **+** *A poena et c.* Near there is the house where Our Lady went to school. A short way on, to the left, is Herod's palace where Christ was led to appear before Herod **+**. Next, a little beyond, is Pilate's house where Christ was bound to the pillar and scourged. On the right is Solomon's Temple where Our Lady, Saint Mary, was married.[58] **+** Nearby is the house of Joachim and Anna, his wife, where Our Lady was born.[59] **+** Close by is a small pool called *Probatica piscina* [the Pool of Sheep], in which many lepers are healed by the virtue of the wood from the Holy Cross which lay in it for many years.[60] A little distance from Solomon's Temple is *Porta Aurea* [the Golden Gate] by which Christ entered the city on Palm Sunday sitting upon a donkey.[61] **+** Close to it is a gate by which Saint Stephen was led out of the city when he was stoned to death. The place where Saint Stephen was stoned is a little way outside the city.[62]

Pilgrimage of the Vale of Jehoshaphat

Not far away in the middle of the Vale of Jehoshaphat is the brook Cedron, where a piece of wood from the Holy Cross was used as a bridge for many years before it was cast into the *Probatica piscina*.[63] In the middle of the Vale of Jehoshaphat is a fair little chapel where there is the sepulchre of Our Lady, Saint Mary. You enter it by going down forty-eight steps. There is an entry fee of three shillings.[64] + A little yonder is a place where Christ prayed to the heavenly Father. Near there is the garden in which Christ was arrested by the Jews after Judas had betrayed Him. A short distance up the way to Mount Olivet is the spot where Christ said to His disciples, "Waken and pray, that ye enter not into temptation".[65] A little further on is the stone where Saint Thomas received the girdle of Our Lady when she ascended into Heaven.[66] A short distance away along the same track is the place where Christ wept over the city of Jerusalem, saying, "There shall not be one stone left upon another". A little yonder is where the angel appeared to Our Lady with the palm saying, "Such a day you shall be taken into heaven".[67] A little beyond is a hill which is called Galilee, where Christ appeared to His Apostles after His Resurrection. There is the place where the children of Israel worshipped Christ when they cast branches of olive in His way.[68] On Mount Olivet is an old temple where Christ ascended into heaven; one can see the footprints in the stone. On Mount Olivet one must pay a fee of two shillings.[69] +

A little yonder is the sepulchre of Pellagia.[70] As you descend the bank you come to an old church where the Apostles composed the Creed. On the same way there is a place where Christ often preached to His Apostles. Also in the same path is the place where Christ taught the Apostles the *Pater Noster* [Our Father].[71] Then comes a place where Our Lady rested every day while visiting the holy places in the Vale of Syloe.[72] Next by the wayside is a place where Saint James the Less was at the time of the Passion and when Christ rose from death to life.[73] Above that is the sepulchre of Zacharias the Just. In the Vale of Syloe is a well where Our Lady washed Our Lord Jesus Christ's clothes when he was a child. A little yonder on the right is Syloe, the *natatoria* [swimming pool], where Christ gave sight to the blind man.[74] Then comes the place where the Prophet Isaiah was sawn in two by a tree-saw. Close to that are the small caves in which the Apostles hid at the time of Jesus Christ's Passion. A little further is a place called Acheldemach which was bought with the thirty pence for which Christ was sold.[75] All Christian pilgrims lie buried there.

Pilgrimage to Mount Syon [76]

A little way from Mount Syon is the place where the Jews tried to seize Our Lady when the Apostles brought her to be buried. Next is the place where Saint Stephen was buried the second time.[77] The east end of the church on Mount Syon is where the holy lamb was prepared. On the north of the church is a stone which Christ stood on when He preached to His disciples. There is another stone which Our Lady sat on when Christ was preaching. Nearby is a spot where Our Lady prayed for fourteen years after Christ's Passion. There too is the place where Our Lady died.+ Close by is a place where Saint John the Evangelist said Mass with Our Lady, Saint Mary.[78] The high altar in the church on Mount Syon is where Christ instituted Maundy with His Apostles. The place where Christ washed His Apostles' feet on Shyr [Maundy] Thursday is to the right of the altar.[79] Outside the church on the south side is a chapel over a vault where the Holy Ghost descended on Whit Sunday,[80] while in the cloister is a small chapel where Saint Thomas of India put his hand to Christ's wound.[81] A short distance from Mount Syon, to the north, was Caiaphas's house, where Christ was in prison. There too is the stone which was put on the sepulchre of Christ to ensure that He should not rise. This place is tended reverently by Greeks.[82] Then comes the place where Saint James the Greater was beheaded and later carried to Spain by the power of Jesus Christ. A chapel of Saint David is on the left. It is seven miles from Jerusalem to Bethlehem.[83]

Pilgrimage to Bethlehem.[84]

On entering the temple everyone must pay a fee of a Venetian groat and another for his donkey-man. In the middle of the temple choir is a chapel, with, as it were, an underground cave, where Jesus Christ was born. This is where Christ was laid between an ox and an ass.[85] To the right of the choir is an altar where the three Kings of Cologne made their offerings. Also in the cloister of the same temple is an underground chapel, to the west. There you will find the study of Saint Jerome, who translated the Bible from Hebrew into Latin, together with his stool. Close by is the sepulchre of the children of Israel [the Holy Innocents].[86] It is seven miles from Bethlehem to Mount Judea where you will see a chapel on the spot where Saint John Baptist was beheaded. There too is the cliff which opened by itself and in which he was hidden.[87] There one pays a Venetian groat. Not far away, thirty steps up, is where Our Lady and Saint Elizabeth met.[88] That is where Our Lady composed the psalm, the *Magnificat*.[89] There is also a fair well where Elizabeth washed Saint John's clothes when he was a baby. Half a mile away is a church where Saint John Baptist was born. Four miles from Mount Judea on the road to Jerusalem is a church where the tree of the Holy Cross grew.[90] It is two miles from there to Jerusalem, where your donkey-man will have a Venetian groat.

Pilgrimage to Bethany.[91]

Two miles east from Jerusalem towards the River Jordan in Bethany is a temple where Saint Lazarus was buried. In the same temple is a small chapel, where Christ stood when He raised that Lazarus from death to life.[92] On entering you will pay a fee of three shillings. In Bethany too is the house of Simon the leper where Christ forgave Mary Magdalene her sins. At the east end of Bethany is the place where Christ rested with His Apostles when Martha said to Him, "Lord, had ye been here Lazarus, my brother, had not been dead."[93] The house of Martha, where Christ often rested, is a little further on together with the house of Mary Magdalene. From Bethany it is twenty-one miles to Mount Quarantina which has a chapel where Christ fasted forty days. The fee there is one shilling. At the top of this mountain is the place where the devil placed Christ and showed Him all the riches of the world and said, "If you will fall down and worship me ye shall have all these riches".[94] Five miles further is the city of Jericho, where Christ often [*gap*]. It is four and a half miles from Jericho to the chapel of Saint John Baptist and half a mile from the River Jordan in which Saint John baptised Christ.[95] The River Jordan runs west into the Dead Sea. It is a fair river but it is always muddy, as if it were troubled. It is near the Dead Sea that Sodom and Gomorrah were stricken and destroyed. In Jerusalem anyone wishing to go to the River Jordan must pay a fee of twelve Venetian groats. His dragoman will cost a further four pence. Then after Rama you must have a guide homewards; that will be another two Venetian groats and two shillings. Everyone has to pay the Sultan two Venetian groats for a safe conduct. As a tip you will give your donkey-man fifteen Venetian groats. Then from Rama to Jaffa on the way home each person will give his donkey-man, by agreement, four Venetian groats and three pence.[96]

On the way home is a city in Lombardy called Mantua, where there is some of Jesus Christ's blood which Longinus brought there together with his spear. Longinus's body also lies there in his sepulchre.[97] Then, in an Abbey on Mount Bernard, is one of Jesus Christ's thorns together with the cheek bone of Saint Bernard.[98] We came home this way through the Duchy of Savoy.

PART 4 - Notes on the Text

1. The Lombards. In the Middle Ages Lombards in particular, together with other Italian merchants, traded through Europe as goldsmiths, money-lenders, pawn-brokers and bankers. In medieval London Lombard Street was their main place of business.

2. Dover. In contrast to Richard of Lincoln (RL), William Wey (WW) took ship in 1462 from Gravesend.

From Calais etc. Both pilgrims travelled across Flanders. WW gives only the distances between places, while RL notes, in addition, the cost of ferries and says which towns and cities had walls.

3. Our Lady's smock. During the Middle Ages pilgrims came in large numbers to venerate "the Great Aachen Relics". These treasures consisted, according to tradition, of Christ's swaddling clothes and loin cloth, the gown of the Virgin and the cloth on which the head of St John the Baptist rested after he was beheaded. Charlemagne received these relics from Jerusalem in 799 and the first pilgrimages to Aachen took place in about 850. The relics, which are now kept in the *Marienschrein* in the cathedral, are put on display every seven years.

There are hot baths. These were known to the Romans who called the place *Aquae Grani*, Granus being the name of a Celtic god of healing. Aachen is still a spa town. The springs are the hottest in central Europe (up to 75 degrees) and are reputedly good for rheumatic conditions. WW refers to *Aquae Grani* in Chapter 11. There he says that in addition to the chemise of the BVM there is also one of Joseph's stockings which is "saffron-coloured, and Christ was placed in it because of the cold when He was lying in the manger". In the same chapter Wey describes how St Helena was said to have found the shift and the swaddling clothes still lying in the manger where the Virgin had dropped them 234 years before. They had remained there because the Jews had forbidden access to the site for the whole of that time.

Aachen is the first town of the Emperor of Germany. WW says "Germany starts".

4. Julich, a little walled town where the Rur runs in front of the town-gate.

5. After Aachen the paths of RL and WW diverge briefly. They converge again at Andernach. Wey went via Duren, Sievernich, Rheinbach and Sinzig. Richard's route was via Cologne where the pilgrim could visit the shrine of the Magi whose relics had been taken from Constantinople to Milan in the fifth century. Frederick Barbarossa removed them from Milan to Cologne in 1162. They are now kept in a magnificent reliquary in Cologne cathedral. From Cologne RL then travelled via Bonn and Remagen to Andernach. This route was three miles longer than Wey's. It is surprising that Wey did not visit the shrine of the Magi and the other relics at Cologne. Perhaps there was a political reason why he did not go there. WW was well aware of the legend which connected the Magi with Cologne. In Chapter 9 he repeats the story that the "Three Kings of Cologne" took ship from Tarsus after visiting Bethlehem to avoid meeting Herod.

The 11,000 Virgins. This is a reference to St Ursula, a 5th-century British princess, who went on pilgrimage to Rome accompanied by 11,000 virgins. All were massacred by the Huns on their return to Cologne.

Another nail figures in RL's account of Milan; (see note 20 below).

St Apollonia, who was martyred in c. 249, was a deaconess of Alexandria. Part of her torture was having all her teeth broken. In art she is often depicted having her teeth pulled out with pincers. She was invoked by those suffering from toothache. Her feast-day was formerly 9th February.

The staff of St Peter is displayed in Cologne Cathedral Treasury.

One of the Children of Israel. Relics of the Holy Innocents, the children murdered on the orders of Herod, (Matthew 2. 16-18), were claimed by a number of churches in England, France and Italy. WW says that there are "many of the Innocents, whose death Herod ordered", in the church of *San Paolo Fuori le Mura* in Rome.

6. A fair walled city and a fair river. The Moselle (Mosel) joins the Rhine at Coblenz. The name of the city is derived from the Latin word for the "confluence" of these two rivers.

7. There (i.e. at Bingen) a river flows into the Rhine. This is the Nahe. Drusus built a wooden bridge over the Nahe which was destroyed in 70AD. It was replaced subsequently by two stone bridges.

A ferry over the water took Richard across the Rhine to the east bank. From Bonn to Bingen all the places he names are on the west bank of the Rhine.

8. A good rest-house. The actual word is "bating house"; cf. the English word "abate". This is one of the more intriguing asides of RL. His narrative is usually plain, factual and unadorned, except when he mentions more important relics and shrines. What was it about this "rest house" between Worms and Speyer which so impressed him?

At Speyer the pilgrims' routes again diverged. WW headed for Ulm while RL continued up the Rhine to Strasburg and Basel.

9. The General Council of all the clergy of Christendom was convoked by Pope Martin V and opened at Basel in 1431. Dissolved by the new Pope, Eugenius IV, in December 1431, the Council disregarded the Pope's action and re-affirmed the Decrees of Constance on the superiority of a General Council over the Pope. In December 1433 the Pope revoked his former decision and recognised the Council. In 1439 the Council was transferred to Ferrara. Those who remained at Basel deposed Pope Eugenius as a heretic and elected Amadeus VIII of Savoy as antipope Felix V. The Council gradually lost its prestige and in 1448 it was driven from Basel and moved to Lausanne where Felix V abdicated. In 1449 it submitted to the legitimate Pope. RL's mention of this Council is important evidence as a *terminus post quem* for his pilgrimage.

In Basel there are still several buildings which Richard could have seen including the

Munster and some half-timbered houses. He could have stayed as a guest in the Franciscan house, the church of which, the *Barfüsser Kirche*, now houses a splendid historical museum.

10. Thrusse. There is no place called "Thrusse" between Basel and Sursee, neither does the traveller cross the Rhine along this route. Richard's description of the length of the route and the destination, however, closely fits Olten which is 24 miles (i.e. 4 Dutch miles) from Basel. Between Basel and Olten the railway now passes through the Hausenstein Tunnel, thus going under Richard's mountains and avoiding the "ill way". The "fair river" at Olten is the Aare, not the Rhine, which is still crossed by a "fair bridge". The handsome medieval, covered bridge has been rebuilt since Richard's time. Now pedestrianised it leads directly to one of the former town gates and customs house. Much of the town wall mentioned by Richard still stands and its line can be easily traced. In the manuscript RL has crossed out the word "village" and substituted the word "town". One can understand why he had some doubt as to whether this settlement should be described as a "village" or a "town".

11. Sursee. The modern name of "Surmare" is Sursee, since the Latin *mare* has been translated into the German *see*. The town is still entered by a gate and some of the medieval walls, including the Mill Tower, where the walls turn a right-angled corner, still stand. Along the line of the former walls there is a row of houses whose gardens occupy the former town moat. In the centre of the town several, originally medieval but since adapted, inns still stand with their handsome wrought-iron signs, e.g. the Sun and the Golden Hind.

12. Lucerne. A long stretch of the wall still stands with nine splendid towers.

There are two oblique medieval bridges, one across the lake and one across the river. The shorter is the *Muhlenbrücke* on the bank of the river Reuss where it rushes out of Lake Lucerne. Its swift flow here was used to power the mill. The longer bridge, here described by Richard, is the *Kapellbrücke*. Only half of this now remains but the length of the original bridge Richard saw is well illustrated in early views of the town and on the engraving in the town's historical museum. Each of these bridges is roofed. The roof of the *Muhlenbrücke* is painted with scenes from the lives of the saints Leodegar and Mauritius and from Swiss history, that of the *Kapellbrücke* with a Dance of Death. The present paintings all date from the 18th century.

Pilgrims on their journeys frequently found a night's lodging with the Friars Minor. Richard could have been received in Lucerne by the Franciscans whose friary was close to the city wall and whose church still stands.

There are still fish in the Reuss, and in the Middle Ages the Fishmarket was very important, occupying a prominent place in the city near the bank of the lake. Its site and history are now marked by a wall plaque.

13. Pilatus Lake. Mount Pilatus, (7000 feet) possibly takes its name from the Latin *pileatus* meaning "capped" (i.e. with cloud) rather than from the Pontius Pilate of the Gospels. One tradition, here repeated by Richard, is that Pilate drowned himself in the small lake here in remorse. (See Eusebius, *Hist. Eccl.* 2.7.)

14. Flüelen. Nowadays it is possible to travel by land from Flüelen on a road built in the 19th century, but we, following Richard, took a boat. It took about three and a half hours to

cross the 23 miles from Lucerne to Flüelen. Richard's distance is again accurate. There is today little of interest in Flüelen, which was, and still is, the disembarkation point for those proceeding to the St Gotthard. The sort of craft used by Richard can be seen in medieval illustrations. The design of the boats employed to cross the lake, using oar and sail as convenient, did not change much until the arrival of the paddle steamer *Stadt Luzern* in 1837. The lake-borne traffic was under the control of a guild of boatmen. Similar powerful guilds appeared on other important medieval waterways; that in Paris was particularly important. Assuming an average speed across the water of between three and four knots Richard would have spent most of one day travelling from Lucerne to Flüelen.

15. Wassen. A bus now runs from Flüelen to Wassen where there is large hotel called the *Hotel Post*. In Richard's time a guild of guides led persons wishing to cross the Alps via the St Gotthard pass from Flüelen to Airolo. In winter oxen were used to trample a path through the snow. The Swiss authorities now make every effort to clear the road of snow by June 1st. We crossed on June 3rd and the snow was still ten feet deep in places at the side of the road. The *Hotel Post* was one of the staging posts where the postillions would change their horses until 1921, when the final horse-drawn mail-coach crossed the St Gotthard pass. In Richard's day there was no surfaced road over the pass and wheeled vehicles could not be used. One may assume that Richard paused for refreshment and a change of mount at the predecessor of the *Hotel Post.*

The approach to Mount Gotthard. At this point there is some confusion in Richard's account. Some of the places he lists are out of order and there are some omissions. From Wassen the next village is Göschenen, where the railway tunnel enters the mountain to emerge on the other side at Airolo. The road to the hospice on the St Gotthard pass proceeds from Göschenen up to Andermatt, where there is now another post hotel called the *Hotel Drei Könige und Post*. The names show that it is an amalgamation of two old hotels. The first, with its reference to the Magi, shows that it was on a pilgrim route to the Three Kings of Cologne. The second name, *Post*, like the one at Wassen, indicates an inn where the post horses were changed and where, even earlier, medieval travellers could change mounts. From Andermatt one now goes to Hospenthal, not mentioned by Richard, where there are a medieval bridge and a tower which were probably there in his time. From Hospenthal the road climbs up to the St Gotthard pass, where there is a hotel/restaurant together with an excellent museum housed in the former hospice buildings.

16. From the hospice the road snakes downward to Airolo, where the railway line emerges from the tunnel and where the mail-coaches changed horses yet again. It continues to Faido, with another post-hotel but little else of interest.

17. Bellinzona, a fair walled town, has three spectacular castles and much of its strongly fortified medieval wall still stands. These together have earned it the status of a World Heritage Site. The strength of its defences shows its importance as the key to the route from Lombardy to Germany.

Other important buildings are the church of *San Biagio* (Saint Blaise) and the Franciscan friary, *Santa Maria della Grazie*, both of which have fine wall paintings. This latter is another Franciscan house where Richard could have stayed on his way to Milan.

18. Mount Syndyr (Mount Cenere in the manuscript) divides the two districts of *Sopprocinere* and *Sottocinere*. The modern traveller by train goes through a long tunnel

under the mountain.

19. The little village at the east end of the water where Richard disembarked is Riva San Vitale. In giving the distance across Lake Lugano to Riva San Vitale Richard seemed to have reverted to English miles. The modern ferries call at Capolago, but in Richard's time passengers disembarked nearby at Riva San Vitale, which is only a few hundred yards from Capolago and is connected it to it by a road on an embankment across reclaimed land. At Riva there is a fine 6th-century Baptistery which was already 800 years old when Richard passed through.

Como. RL's fair water is Lake Como.

20. One of the nails that were driven into Christ's hand. In Milan Cathedral a large crucifix, suspended high above the chancel, is believed to contain a nail from Christ's cross, which was re-worked to become the bit for the bridle of the Emperor Constantine's horse. The crucifix is lowered once a year, on September 14, the Feast of the Cross, by a device invented by Leonardo da Vinci. Another nail, in Cologne, is mentioned by RL see note 5 above.

21. Pavia. Medieval Pavia was known as the city of a hundred towers. In the Dark Ages it was the capital of the Kingdom of the Lombards. Several German emperors received the traditional iron crown of the Lombard kings in the church of St Michael. In the 14th century the city was handed to the Viscontis and became a satellite of Milan. The Archpoet gives an indication of Pavia's reputation in the 12th century in the line,

> *Quis Paviae demorans castus habeatur?*
> Who may be considered chaste if he dwells in Pavia?

22. The fair park. The *Certosa di Pavia* is ten kilometers from Pavia. It is the site of an important Carthusian monastery, commissioned in 1396 by Gian Galeazzo Visconti. The monastery lies in what had been a vast Visconti hunting range which stretched all the way to the *castello* in Pavia. Presumably this is the park referred to by RL who passed the site while the monastery, which took 100 years to build, was still under construction. The refectory is divided by a blind wall which allowed the monastery to feed pilgrims staying in their guest house without compromising the rules of the closed order. The building of the church began in 1453, the year before RL's pilgrimage.

23. Saint Augustine. The white marble tomb of St Augustine is in Pavia's St Peter's church (*San Pietro in Ciel d'Oro*). The well can still be seen in the crypt. RL, as a doctor, was interested in holy sites which had therapeutic powers, cf. his mention of Longinus's spear on p. 13.

24. The river which enters the Po is the Ticino, which flows into Lake Maggiore from the north and out of it from the south. Here pilgrims who had arrived on foot or on horseback generally continued the rest of their journey to Venice by river or canal, leaving their horses with friends or an inn-keeper to await their return (see M. Newett, *Canon Casola's Pilgrimage*, p. 351, note 7).

25. There Roland was the captain. The columns of the Gothic porch of Cremona Cathedral rest on two lions; their capitals represent Roland sounding his horn on one side and

Charlemagne on the other. For another mention of Roland see note 29 below.

26. To Venice, all by water. Having come down the river from Pavia, RL sailed across the Venetian lagoon to Venice.

The church of *Sant'Elena*, founded in the early 13th century and rebuilt in 1435, shortly before Richard's visit, was abandoned in 1807 but reopened in 1928. The body of Saint Helena, mother of Constantine the Great, could be seen until recently in a glass case under the altar in a small chapel on the south side. It has now been moved for safety while refurbishment takes place. Some medieval chroniclers claimed that Saint Helena was a British princess, the daughter of King Coel. Although erroneous, the story was attractive to English pilgrims.

St Zacharias's relics are preserved in the church of *San Zaccaria*. The original ninth-century church, rebuilt between the 10th and 12th centuries, was restructured between 1444 and 1515. WW mentions both of these churches.

The bone of St Christopher and one of the arms of St George. WW writes, "On Marianus... in St George's church there is St Christopher's leg bone which is very long".

St Gregory, c. 540-604 was Pope from 590. Gregory the Great was the fourth and last of the traditional Latin "Doctors of the Church". Bede tells the famous story of his encounter with the fair-haired Saxon slaves in the market, "*non Angli, sed angeli.*" His book, *Liber Regulae Pastoralis*, was translated by King Alfred and became the textbook of the medieval episcopate.

St Theophilus (later second century) was Bishop of Antioch and one of the "Christian Apologists". Of his writings only his *Apology* has survived.

WW does not mention the bodies of St Gregory or St Theophilus, although he does list the relics of more than 50 other saints.

The Cathedral is the famous *Basilica di San Marco*, completed in 1094. It has been embellished over the centuries since then. The body of St Mark was stolen from Alexandria and brought to Venice in 828. RL's brief description is very different from WW's enthusiastic list of what he saw in the basilica.

27. A man must board his galley... and pay for his passage. WW's account is much more detailed. He devotes the whole of his Chapter 2, *A Provision*, to the arrangements which must be made with the "patron". This chapter is in English and is repeated in Latin in Chapter 9 where it forms part of WW's long account of his five-week stay in the city, from 22 April to 26 May, 1462. The fare is the same as that stated by RL, 40 ducats and to be at the patron's board, "if you are to get a good place and be comfortable in the galley and be well looked after... and for your meat and drink to the port of Jaffa and back to Venice". WW then goes on to give details of the route, the distances between ports and the conditions of carriage which are part of the contract between pilgrim and patron. Next he offers very detailed, not to say homely, advice about the kit, provisions, condiments and medications which the pilgrim should purchase in Venice for himself and his servant "if you have one". Two examples may be given of Wey's solicitude and the amount of detail he gives:-

"You should also buy in Venice a small chamber pot, because if you become ill and are unable to climb to the upper parts of the galley, you will be able to do what you have to in it."

and

"You can buy a set of bed-clothes in Venice near St Mark's. For three ducats you will get a feather bed, a mattress, two pillows, two pairs of small linen sheets and a small quilt. When you return to the seller in Venice he will take them back and give you one and a half ducats for the set of bedding." This transaction is referred to by RL when he writes, "the bed will cost you another ducat and a half".

28. St Euphemia, according to tradition, was a Christian from Chalcedon in Asia Minor, who was martyred in the reign of Diocletian. After surviving various other tortures she was thrown to the lions. Her sixth-century sarcophagus, which was brought here from Constantinople in 800 AD to keep it safe from the Iconoclasts, is now displayed in a small sanctuary in St Euphemia's church.

29. Roland's Palace and Tower. There are several Roman buildings in Pula, the most striking being the immense amphitheatre. Did RL's informant perhaps attribute this to Roland? There is another mention of Roland in note 25.

The statue of a knight on top of a small column in St Blaise's Square in Dubrovnik (Ragusa), known as Orlando's column, was erected in 1418. Although the cult of Roland was primarily a North European one, the legend was adopted by Ragusa which made him the city's saviour in battles against the Saracens. The real Saracen siege of Ragusa occurred a century after Roland's death. Neither RL nor WW mentions this monument.

30. Zadar. WW also mentions Jarra (Zadar) on his return journey in 1458 and speaks of St Simeon, St Zoyolus and St Anastasia. He again mentions Simeon in connexion with Jarra on the 1462 outward voyage. Wey says that Zoyolus and Simeon are in the same church and Anastasia is in the cathedral. Richard, however, puts Anastasia in the minster of Zoyolus. At the present time the splendid reliquary casket of Simeon is in his own church, that of Anastasia is in her Cathedral and Zoyolus's skull is displayed in the permanent exhibition of religious art in the convent beside St Mary's Church. RL is incorrect in saying that Anastasia was (present) at the birth of Christ. WW explains the reason for the confusion. It arose because her feast day is on the anniversary of her martyrdom, 25th December. According to tradition she died in about 304 at Sirmium in Pannonia.

St Simeon is credited with composing the *Nunc dimittis* (Luke 2, vv 29-32). It has formed part of daily prayers since the 4th century. It features in Evensong in the *Book of Common Prayer* starting with the words, "Lord, now lettest thou thy servant depart in peace...".

St Zoyolus. A St Zoilus is believed to have been martyred under Diocletian in c.301 in Córdoba. There was another saint, however, named Zoellus, who was probably martyred in Istria, and he may be the one commemorated here.

31. From Zadar...to Korčula. There is a gap in RL's text here, where the name of the place 100 miles from Zadar and 50 miles before Korčula is omitted. WW gives the name of the

intermediate port which he visited as Sesule.

32. Ragusa is now known as Dubrovnik. Our word "argosy", derived from Ragusa, commemorates its trading reputation. RL's comment on Dubrovnik is very slight, mentioning only its wealth and its wall. WW, like RL, mentions these two features but also records that the arm of St Blaise is there. He adds that the "silver money there is very good". The reliquary containing the arm of St Blaise is displayed at present in the Treasury in the cathedral.

33. Durres and Corfu. WW reports that Durres was the home station for 16 Venetian galleys whose task was to guard Venetian interests in the Adriatic.

According to WW, St Arsenius was buried in Corfu.

The miracle in the chapel of the BVM at Cassiopi is also related by WW, who adds the curious detail that the town had been destroyed by a crocodile.

WW, like RL, gives the distance from Corfu to Methoni as 300 miles. WW twice mentions the "Romney wine" which grows here.

34. St Leo, the holy hermit. Wey also mentions the shrine of St Leo, describing him as a martyr. Canon Casola was shown the body of St Leo when he called at Methoni in 1494. There is a problem with RL's words "to the south a mile from the town". Methoni is on the coast, and a mile south of the town would place the shrine in the sea. There is, in fact, a rather small, disused Byzantine church in the middle of a small-holding a couple of miles north of the town, which local people (in 2000) claimed to be dedicated to St Leo.

35. Both writers agree on the subsequent distances i.e. from Methoni to Cande (Herakleion) as 300 miles, and from Cande to Rhodes as another 300 miles. WW is more forthcoming about Crete than is RL. He mentions King Minos and St Paul's adventure there (*see* Titus 1.12). On his return visit WW describes how he saw the head of Titus, who had been archbishop of Gortyn, and notes that mallasetum (Malmsey), cypress and sugar are grown there. WW also mentions some "old" documents concerning St George which he found in Cande. It is tempting to think that WW found these in the famous library of the Franciscan friary where he might have stayed for a few days. This library is undergoing restoration at present to become a museum in Herakleion.

Rhodes made a strong impression on both pilgrims. Each of them describes the thorn from Christ's crown and the way it flowers on Good Friday. WW's 1458 description of it is as brief as RL's. In 1462, however, WW gives a very much more detailed account, which involves two thorns, one of which produces a flower which changes colour miraculously as the account of the Passion is read. On this visit too WW describes the great hospital of the Knights. On his return to Rhodes in August 1462 Wey writes about the famous icon of Our Lady of Philerimos, something which RL does not mention. This icon, together with the hand of John the Baptist, were the two most treasured possessions of the Knights Hospitaller and accompanied them on their relocation to Malta. After many further adventures they are now in the old Montenegrin capital of Cetinje. RL refers to the hand of St Katherine whereas WW mentions only the hand of the Baptist.

36. Skyr Thursday is an old name for Maundy Thursday. Perhaps the name is derived from "skere" or "sheer" meaning "clear" of "free from guilt", and refers to the practice of receiving absolution or, alternatively, of ceremonially washing the altars of the church on that day. RL uses the word again; see note 79 below.

37. Both RL and WW give the distance from Rhodes to Jaffa as 700 miles. WW includes the intermediate distance to Paphos in Cyprus; i.e. Rhodes to Paphos 400 miles and Paphos to Jaffa 300 miles.

38. The stone on which St Peter stood. WW's words are almost identical, *Unum miliare a Jaffa, iam infra mare, est petra magna ubi Sanctus Petrus stabat olim ad piscandum*; "One mile from Jaffa is the great rock where St Peter used to stand to fish, it is now beneath the sea."

39. There you must hire a donkey. And from Jaff ten miles to Rama. WW writes, *Nos peregrini accipiebamus asinos ad equitandum Rame, quae distat a Jaff decem miliaria Wallica*; "We pilgrims took our asses to ride to Rama which is 10 Welsh miles from Jaffa."

40. The city of Lydda where St George was martyred. WW gives much more detail, "… to the town of Lydda, but which was once called Diaspolis. At one time it was a great city but now it is almost in ruins; it is in the land of the Philistines. Pilgrims make their offerings to St George in the church of the Greeks. This used to be large and beautiful but now for the greater part it is in ruins. St George was martyred there." *Ibi sanctus Georgius marterizatus*.

41. Rama was the birthplace of Joseph of Arimathaea who begged the body of Jesus from Pilate and buried Him in his own sepulchre, (Matthew 27.57; Mark 15.43; Luke 23.50; John 19.38). Ramathaim-zophim, in Ephraim, was the home of Samuel (1.Samuel 1.19). It was also known as Ramah and, in New Testament times, as Arimathaea.

42. Where you see the sign of the cross etc. This convention is also used by WW. RL's words are an almost exact translation of William Wey's:- *Ubi ponitur crux est plena indulgentia a pena et culpa, ubi non ponitur crux sunt indulgentie septem annorum et septem quadragenarum dierum. Predicte indulgentie concesse fuerunt a sancto Silvestro Papa ad preces sancti et magni Constantini imperatoris et sancte Helene matris ejus.* This is the most striking similarity between the narratives of the two pilgrims and one suspects that these identical quotations come from a common source, perhaps one supplied by the Franciscan guides.

St Silvester was Bishop of Rome from 314 to 335. According to legend he cleansed Constantine the Great from leprosy and baptized him on his death bed. In fact Constantine was baptized after the death of Silvester.

Constantine the Great (c. 274-337) was proclaimed Emperor at York in 306. He defeated his rival, Maxentius, at the Battle of the Milvian Bridge in 312. He established his capital at Byzantium, which he renamed Constantinople, in 330. He shares a feast day, 21 May, with his mother St Helena. See note 26.

43. Saint Samuel, the prophet. See note note 41.

The Castle of Emmaus. WW also visited this site, "Beside the road on the right, in the mountains, was the church which was once called Emmaus Castle, where the two disciples recognized Christ in the breaking of bread". Luke 24.18 gives the name of one of them as Cleophas. Some traditions say that this Cleophas was the husband of Mary. See note below.

44. Saint Mary Cleophas. One of the women who stood by the cross (John 19.25). Some have identified her with Mary the wife of Alphaeus (Cleophas) and mother of James the Less (Mark 3.18 and 15.40).

Stone of white alabaster. This stone is also noted by WW who says that it is about one and a half feet long and is engraved with many crosses.

45. Christ's Temple, called by WW the "Church of the Holy Sepulchre". While WW does not record the fees payable by pilgrims, he does explain that hours of admission were strictly controlled by the Saracens. Christian pilgrims were only allowed in at nightfall. The Saracens counted them and noted their names. The pilgrims remained in the church all night, accompanied by Franciscan monks, and had to leave the next morning. RL's description of the three entry fees implies that he made three visits. WW, similarly, describes the three nights his group spent in the church.

There is on the south side of the temple a chapel where Christ first appeared to His Mother after His Resurrection and said "*Salve sancta parens.*" WW's account, however, says, "The Chapel of the Most Blessed Virgin Mary is on the north. There Christ is believed to have appeared after His Resurrection to His Most Blessed Mother on Easter Day." Canon Casola does not state which side the chapel was on. (Newett; *Canon Casola's Pilgrimage*, p. 258)

Christ was beaten with scourges in Pilate's house. See Matthew 27.2; Mark 15.15; John 19.1. The pillar is often shown on the "Symbols of the Passion".

46. Caiaphas's house. The events in Caiaphas's house are described in Matthew 27.57-75; Mark 14.53-72; Luke 22.54-71 and John 18.12-27.

47. In the middle of the chapel is a round stone of various colours where St Helena verified the Cross upon which Christ died by raising a dead man to life. WW's version is similar, "In the middle of this chapel lies a round, marble stone. On this stone they placed a corpse and then laid the three crosses on top of it. When Christ's cross was placed on the dead woman's body, she, who was previously dead, immediately rose up". According to legend, St Helena found the crosses of Christ and the two thieves on Golgotha. The true one was identified by the miracle described by RL and WW. The Veneration of the Cross at Jerusalem is first described in the fourth-century *Pilgrimage of Etheria*. Until 1960 a church festival commemorating the discovery was held on 3 May.

48. The stone with a hole and *Noli me tangere*. The meeting of Mary Magdalene with the risen Christ is described in John 20.15-17. WW also describes the stone with a hole, "A round stone of white marble veined with black. It contains a hole in the centre three fingers long. When Our Lord appeared to St Mary Magdalene on the Day of Resurrection in the guise of a gardener He made that hole in the afore-said stone with the spade which was in His hand, and said to Mary, "Do not touch me," John 20.17.

49. The Jews diced… Matthew 27.27-35 and Mark 15.16 describe this event. Both Gospel writers describe those who impressed Simon of Cyrene and later diced for Christ's seamless garment as "soldiers". They would have been part of the Roman garrison, not Jews, as RL says. WW, who knew the Gospels well, would not have made this error. In perpetuating these examples of anti-Semitic propaganda, RL, who was not as familiar with the Bible as WW was, was probably repeating misinformation given by the guide.

50. There is a chapel down 32 steps where St Helena found the Cross. WW says, "there is a flight of 29 steps leading down to the chapel of St Helena. Inside this chapel there is another flight of 10 steps down to a pit, where were discovered Christ's holy cross, the nails and the point of the lance, which had been hidden together with the thieves' crosses. Casola (*op. cit.* p.260) merely says "several steps". See also the note on St Helena and the Invention of the Cross, above.

51. In the same temple, is a pillar where Jesus Christ was spat upon and crowned with thorns. WW has, "Outside that entrance to St Helena's chapel, on the left, is an altar under which is a column, about one ell long, on which Jesus sat when He was crowned with thorns in Pilate's house". (Matthew 27.29; Mark 15.17; John 19.2)

52. There is a crack in the rock face which split when Christ yielded the ghost. Matthew 27.51; Mark 16.38 and Luke 23.45 all describe this event. WW writes, "About five feet away from here, towards the south, is that cleft of which it is said, "And the rocks were rent". This is one and a half palms in length and four feet long. It runs east and west."

53. The angel said to the three Marys, "Whom seek ye?" In the *Vulgate* Luke 24.5 has the angel, speaking to the three women, saying, "*Quid quaeritis viventem cum mortuis?*" ("Why do you (plural) seek the living among the dead?") John 20.15 has Christ, speaking to Mary Magdalene alone, using the words "*Quem quaeris?*" ("Whom do you (singular) seek?") RL, or his guide, has conflated the two questions.

54. In the temple is a hole in a stone where Christ said to His Disciples, "Here is the midst of the world". In most medieval *Mappae Mundi*, Jerusalem was placed in the centre as *omphalos*, or navel, of the earth. One of the origins of this tradition is to be found in Ezekiel 5.5, "Thus saith the Lord God: This is Jerusalem: I have set it in the mist of the nations and countries that are round about her".

55. There is a chapel where the sepulchre of Adam is. WW writes, in Chapter 7, "There is an altar on the spot where Adam's head was discovered". In his Chapter 6 he gives more detail, "There is a hole for the Cross in white marble tinged with red flecks. Adam's head was found in that hole after the Flood as a sign that therein lay redemption. On that stone is written, 'Here God achieved salvation in the midst of the earth'." A tradition, first found in Origen, placed Adam's tomb on Calvary so that at the Crucifixion the blood of the Second Adam was poured over the head of the First.

56. "Woman see your son". These words were spoken by Jesus to Mary and St John as they stood by the Cross; John 19.26.

57. The Stations without the Temple. From early times pilgrims in Jerusalem followed the *Via Dolorosa*, the traditional route taken by Christ from Pilate's house to Calvary. On their

return home they often replicated the route by a series of pictures or carvings round the walls of a church which illustrated episodes from Christ's last journey. As an act of devotion they visited these "Stations" in order, reciting prayers and meditating on each incident. In the Middle Ages the Franciscans, who provided guides for pilgrims in Jerusalem, popularized this, but the final selection of incidents was not made until the 18th and 19th centuries. The progress now usually consists of 14 Stations.

The Jews constrained Simon to take the Cross. Nowadays this is depicted as the fifth Station. The incident is described by Matthew 27.32; Mark 15.21 and Luke 23.26. Both Matthew and Mark describe those who impressed Simon as "soldiers". In saying that those concerned were "Jews" RL is reproducing anti-Semitic propaganda. See note 49 on "The Jews diced".

58. The Temple of Solomon. The first Temple dated from the reign of Solomon (c.970-933 BC). This was destroyed in 586 BC. The second Temple was begun in 520 BC but suffered desecration. The grandest Temple was built by Herod the Great, who ruled from 37 to 4 BC.

59. Joachim and Anna. Many details which were later incorporated in the story of Joachim and Anna are to be found in the books of the "Apocryphal New Testament", the *Gospel of the Birth of Mary* and the *Protoevangelion of James*. Joachim is described as a rich, childless man, who was despised by the high priest, Issachar, for his childlessness and "confounded with the shame of such reproach, retired to the shepherds, who were with their cattle in their pastures". His wife, Anna, however, eventually conceived a child, Mary. Apart from these passages he is rarely referred to in Christian writings until several centuries later – in the East seldom before the seventh century and in the West not until the Middle Ages, when he became a frequent subject for religious artists. (See note on *Porta Aurea* below.)

St Anne's name is not found in the Bible. The legendary events of her life, like those of her husband, Joachim, appear in the *Gospel of the Birth of Mary* and in the *Protoevangelion of James*. Her cult developed later, especially in Brittany, of which she became the patron saint.

60. *Probatica piscina,* "which is called in the Hebrew tongue Bethesda," John 5.2. This pool was believed to possess healing properties associated with a periodical disturbance of the water. WW also visited the site and says, "An angel stirred the water once each day". Cf, John 2.4. *Probata* is the Greek for "sheep", hence the phrase used in the *Vulgate* for the "pool by the sheep market". (*Gospel of Nicodemus* 5.14)

Porta Aurea means "The Golden Gate". This is mentioned in the *Gospel of the Birth of Mary* 2.13. "And this shall be a sign to you of the things which I declare, namely, when you come to the Golden Gate of Jerusalem, you shall there meet your wife, Anna, who being very much troubled that you returned no sooner, shall then rejoice to see you." In the *Protoevangelion* 4.4. we read, "Anna stood by the gate and saw Joachim coming with the shepherds".

61. Christ entered the city on Palm Sunday sitting on a donkey. The events are described in Matthew 21.1-11; Mark 11.1-11 and Luke 19. 29-38. See also John 12.12-15.

62. Saint Stephen was stoned to death. The stoning of Stephen is described in Acts 7. 58-60.

63. Vale of Jehoshaphat. On the basis of Joel 3.2 and 12, the Valley of Jehoshaphat was the traditional scene of the Lord's Coming Judgement. For the death of Jehoshaphat see 1 Kings 22.50 and 2 Chronicles 21.1. Some of the faithful in the Middle Ages were worried that there might not be sufficient room in the valley on the Day of Judgement for all those who will rise from the dead, and it is on record that one German asked a pilgrim to the Holy Land to reserve a place for him by depositing a stone with his name written on it in the Valley.

64. A fair little chapel in the which is the sepulchre of Our Lady, Saint Mary. It is instructive to compare WW's account, "In the valley of Jehoshaphat, on the right, there is a large chapel of the Virgin Mary. On its eastern side, beneath a well-made chapel, is her tomb, beautifully decorated with stones of white marble. This chapel has one entrance to the south. There is a flight of 48 steps leading from that entrance to the floor of the chapel." While WW gives much more detail of the building, he does not mention the entrance fee, of three shillings, which RL, typically, does.

65. The place where Christ prayed. WW also visited this spot and describes it as, "a large stone cave where Christ prayed three times to the Father on the night of the Last Supper, and His sweat was like drops of blood dripping to the ground; Luke 22.44.

The garden in which Christ was taken by the Jews after Judas had betrayed Him. The betrayal by Judas and Christ's arrest are described in Matthew 26. 47-49; Mark 14. 43-46 and Luke 22.47.

Christ said to His Disciples, "Waken and pray, that ye enter not into temptation." The agony in the garden is described in Matthew 26.41 and Mark 14.38. In both Gospels the *Vulgate* uses the words,"*Vigilate et orate ut non intretis in tentationem*," which RL translates literally here.

66. St Thomas received the girdle of Our Lady. The belief in the bodily Assumption of the Blessed Virgin is first met with in later fourth-century New Testament apocrypha. In 1950 Pope Pius XII declared the Corporal Assumption a dogma of the Roman Catholic Church. The scene of Mary on her death-bed surrounded by the Apostles is often depicted in art as the "Dormition". In the Eastern Church it is called the *Koimesis*. Many legends grew up about the events which occurred at the time of the Virgin's death. One tells how the Apostles were miraculously reunited, some from very far afield, to be present at Mary's death. Thomas arrived typically late and expressed incredulity at what the others told him. To convince him the Virgin dropped her girdle to him from Heaven.

According to WW the girdle was preserved in the castle of Pratus, 10 miles from Florence, "*Cingulum beatissime Mariae, quod miserat sancto Thome Indie, in monte Oliveti, est in castello Prati, decem miliaria a Florentia*". At present the girdle is kept in the late 14th-century chapel of the Holy Girdle in Prato Cathedral. Agnolo Gaddi (died 1396) covered the walls of this chapel with frescoes illustrating the legend and, probably in the 1430's, Donatello and Michelozzo created the outdoor pulpit of the Holy Girdle from which it is displayed to the faithful five times a year.

Jesus wept upon the city of Jerusalem saying, "There shall not be one stone left upon another." Matthew 24.2 and Mark 13.2, in the *Vulgate*, both have "*non relinquetur lapis super lapidem*". (See also Luke 19.41-44 and 21.6.)

67. Where the angel appeared to Our Lady with the palm saying, "Such a day you shall be taken into heaven". The *Golden Legend* describes various events connected with the death of the Virgin. She was warned of her death by Gabriel who brought her a palm, not, as at the Annunciation, a lily. WW, on his *Mappa Terrae Sanctae*, gives the location of this episode as Mount Olivet, "*Palma adducta ad beatissimam Virginem per angelum in monte Oliveti*". See also note above on the girdle of the BVM.

68. The hill called Galilee where Christ appeared to His Disciples after His Resurrection. See Matthew 26.32; 28.7,10 and 16-17.

The children of Israel did worship to Christ when they cast branches of olive trees in His way. See note 61.

69. Mount Olivet where Christ ascended into heaven, and one can see the footprints on the stone. One of the sights shown to pilgrims was the stone showing Christ's footprints made as He ascended. WW describes it thus, "On the stone, which is of white marble, there remains the imprint of Christ's right foot". In the Middle Ages a stone in Westminster Abbey was also said to bear such a mark. This duplication presented the faithful with a problem. WW refers to it on two other occasions, "*Utrum vestigia pedum Christi ascendentis in celum sint in monte Oliveti? Respondetur, quod sunt vestigia duorum pedum Christi in lapide duro, sed dextrum vestigium potest manifestius videri*", (Chapter 9). In Chapter 11 WW writes, "*Pars dextri vestigii pedis Christi monstratur in die Ascensionis apud Westmonasterium.*" There used to be an interesting, mid 15th-century, Nottingham alabaster panel in Wells Cathedral which depicted the Ascension and the imprint of Christ's feet.

70. Sepulchre of Pellagia. According to legend, St Pellagia, the Penitent, was an actress who was converted at Antioch. Dressing as a man she then travelled to Jerusalem where she lived a life of penance.

71. Where Christ taught the Apostles the *Pater Noster*. The Lord's Prayer is recorded in Matthew 6.9-13 and Luke 11.2-4.

72. Where Our Lady rested every day while visiting the holy places of the Vale of Syloe. Four years later WW's guide told him the same story in similar words, "The place where the Blessed Virgin Mary rested because she was tired when she was visiting these holy places."

73. A place where St James the Less was at the time of the Passion and when Christ was risen from death to life. WW writes, "The spot where Christ appeared to St James the Less on the Day of Resurrection and set bread before him saying, Rise, my brother, and eat". St James the Less, the son of Alphaeus, was one of the Twelve. Some traditions identify him with the St James, the Lord's brother, who became the first Bishop of Jerusalem, and was martyred in 62 by being thrown from the pinnacle of the Temple and then stoned to death. He is represented also as the author of the apocryphal *Book of James*, the *Protoevangelion*, from which were drawn the stories of Joachim and Anna and some of the legends about the BVM.

74. The Sepulchre of Zacharias the Just. WW writes, "Zacharias, the son of Barachias, was buried in the same place. He was slain between the temple and the altar." According to the *Protoevangelion* (16.9-16), Zacharias, husband of Elizabeth and father of John the Baptist, was murdered in the Temple at the command of Herod during the Massacre of the Innocents when the whereabouts of his son were not revealed. See also note 87, on the miraculous concealment of the infant St John at this time.

A well where Our Lady washed Our Lord, Jesus Christ's, clothes. WW's account follows that of RL very closely here as their guides plainly escorted their parties along a traditional route. WW's description is more picturesque, "On the other side of the bridge of Syloe is the way down into a dell hidden in a valley at the bottom of which is a spring with excellent water. The Most Blessed Mary washed the clothes of her son, Jesus, there when she presented Him in the Temple."

Syloe, where Christ gave sight to the blind man. For the story of the blind man and the pool of Siloam (Syloe) see John 9.7 and 11. It is notable that RL here uses the actual word *natatoria*, "swimming pool", which occurs in the *Vulgate.*

75. The prophet Isaiah was sawn in two. The martyrdom of Isaiah, by being cut in two by a wood-saw, is described in the second-century composite Jewish-Christian work, *The Ascension of Isaiah.* There may be a reference to this episode in Hebrews 11.37.

The small caves where the Apostles hid at the time of the Passion. The flight of the Disciples is noted in Matthew 26.56.

The place called Alcheldemach that was bought for 30 pennies. See Matthew 27. 7-10 with Zechariah 11, 12 and 13, and Acts 1,18 and 19.

76. Pilgrimages of Mount Syon. This is one of RL's five sub-titles, the full list being:-

        Pilgrimages in the city of Jerusalem
        Pilgrimages in the Vale of Jehoshaphat
        Pilgrimage on Mount Syon
        Pilgrimage in Bethlehem
        Pilgrimage in Bethany

WW's rather longer list, with some similar sub-titles, is:-

        Pilgrimages to the sites of the Stations
        Pilgrimages in the Valley of Jehoshaphat
        Pilgrimages on Mount Olivet
        Other Pilgrimages in the Valley of Jehoshaphat
        Pilgrimages in the Valley of Siloe
        Pilgrimages on Mount Syon
        Pilgrimages and the Holy Sites in the Church of the Holy Sepulchre
        Pilgrimages on the road to Bethlehem

Pilgrimages within the Site and Church at Bethlehem
Pilgrimages outside Bethlehem
Pilgrimages in the Mountains of Judaea
Pilgrimages from Jerusalem to Jordan
Pilgrimages in Bethany

These two lists are interesting in that they show the route devised and followed by the Franciscans as they conducted their pilgrim groups around Jerusalem and the Holy Land. While WW tells his reader where the pilgrims spent each night, in varying degrees of discomfort, RL makes no mention of domestic arrangements. He does, however, show how expensive the pilgrimage was in terms of entrance fees, bribes and gratuities – an aspect almost completely ignored by WW. Christian pilgrims must have been irked at having to pay fees to the Saracens to visit their holy places, quite apart from their intrusive bureaucracy, exemplified in roll-calls and inconvenient admission times.

77. **The place where the Jews tried to seize Our Lady when the Apostles brought her to be buried.** According to tradition, at the death of the Virgin her soul, in the form of a child, was received by Christ himself. While her body was being taken for burial a certain Hebrew, named Jephonias, tried to seize it. His hands stuck to the bier (or were cut off) until he repented and St Peter freed him. WW shows the location of this episode in the index to his *Mappa* with the words, *Locus ubi Judaei voluerunt rapuisse corpus beatissimae Virginis.* On the third day the Archangel Michael accompanied her body to Paradise where it was reunited with her soul. She left behind an empty tomb, later found by the Apostles to be filled with roses and lilies. According to one version this was the point at which St Thomas, who had arrived too late to witness the Assumption himself in company with the other Apostles, typically refused to believe the miracles which had occurred. Thereupon the Virgin appeared to him in a vision and herself dropped her girdle from Heaven into his hands.

78. **Where St Stephen was buried the second time.** St Stephen, the protomartyr, was stoned to death, according to Acts 7.60. He was buried by "devout men" (Acts 8.2), but the site of his tomb was not known until discovered by Lucian in 415. From the end of the fourth century his feast has been kept on 26 December. A second feast, *Inventio S. Stephani,* commemorating the finding of his relics, is also kept, on 3 August. He was one of the most popular saints of the Middle Ages.

Where the holy lamb was roasted. WW was shown the place "where the Paschal Lamb was prepared for the Lord's supper". (See Mark 14.12)

Various stones and places on Mt Syon. Many of these places were pointed out also to WW. The two lists are not identical but reflect the interests and knowledge of the two men. Both mention the place where Our Lady died (see note above) and also the place where St John is said to have celebrated Mass for the Virgin.

79. **Where Christ washed His Apostles' feet upon Maundy Thursday.** See note 36. Shyr Thursday is Maundy Thursday. The event is described in John 13.5-12.

80. **The Holy Ghost descended on Whit Sunday.** For Pentecost see Acts 2.1-36.

81. Where St Thomas of India put his hand to Christ's wound. Described by WW, "One goes down into the cloister in the corner of which there is a small chapel to St Thomas. There Christ offered Himself to St Thomas to be touched, and it is where Jesus entered although the doors were closed". (John 20 26-28)

A tradition, derived from the Gnostic *Acts of Thomas*, asserts that Thomas brought the Gospel to India where he was martyred. It was believed that he was buried at Mulapore near Madras, but his relics are now supposed to be at Ortona in the Abruzzi.

82. Caiaphas's house where Christ was in prison. The events in the House of Caiaphas are described in Matthew 27.57-75; Mark 14.53-72; Luke 22.54-71 and John 18.12-27. See note 46.

A stone which was put on the sepulchre of Christ. WW writes of this stone in more detail, "A stone's throw to the north is the Church of Our Saviour. Armenians minister there. On the high altar of this church lies that stone which was rolled to the mouth of Jesus' tomb; it is really large, being more than two fathoms long and one and a half thick. It is made of white marble." (See Mark 15.46)... "This church used to be the House of Caiaphas." The two pilgrims differ here in their accounts of which nation was responsible for this site. WW says that the "Armenians minister there", while RL says that it is "kept by the Greeks". Later in his Chapter 7 WW says that there were 12 sects responsible for various sites in the Temple, which may explain why some pilgrims became confused.

83. St James the Greater was beheaded and, according to tradition, later carried to Spain. WW writes of this site, "There is a small chapel on the east side of this (the Armenians' church) where the Apostle, St James, the brother of St John the Evangelist, was beheaded by Herod". The death of St James the Greater is mentioned in Acts 12.2. There was an ancient tradition that after his death the body of St James was transported miraculously in a stone boat to Galicia, in north-west Spain. After several centuries and various vicissitudes it found its final resting place in Compostella where it became the goal of one of the three great pilgrimages of the Middle Ages. The casket containing the relics of St James may be seen today beneath the high altar of the Cathedral of Santiago de Compostela.

A Chapel of St David. Today the Tomb of King David on Mount Zion is beneath the hall of the Last Supper, on the lower floor of the large church built by the Crusaders to commemorate Mary's Dormition.

It is seven miles to Bethlehem. WW writes, "It is five miles south from Jerusalem to Bethlehem." While there are hardly any discrepancies in the distances given by RL and WW in the earlier sections of their pilgrimages, some differences appear once they are in the Holy Land.

84. Pilgrimage of Bethlehem. See note 76. WW, unlike RL, describes several sites between Jerusalem and Bethlehem which had significant links with the Old Testament figures of Elijah, Jacob and Rachel. He also mentions the fact that pilgrims were accommodated in the cloister of the Franciscan house in Bethlehem and that they were escorted around the various sites by the monks.

A Venice groat and a penny. See note 92 on currency and fees.

85. A Chapel with, as it were, a cave where Jesus Christ was born. The manger is described in Luke 2.7. The ox and the ass, which are also mentioned by WW, do not feature in the Gospels. They probably come from Isaiah's words, "The ox knoweth his owner and the ass his master's crib", Isaiah 1.3.

The Three Kings of Cologne. For the visit of the Magi see Matthew 2.1-11. The Magi were considered as the proto-pilgrims. Their shrine at Cologne, see note 5 above, was an important place of pilgrimage in its own right.

86. The study of St Jerome who translated the Bible from Hebrew into Latin. WW writes, "The pilgrims go first into the cloister on the north side of the church. There is a flight of 18 steps there, on the east, called St Jerome's Staircase, which leads down to the chapel. There is a place in the wall where he used to sit when he translated the Bible from Hebrew into Latin. He used to celebrate Mass in the same chapel. There is also the place where he used to sleep and where he was later buried. His body has now been translated to the church of Santa Maria Maggiore in Rome."

St Jerome (c.342-420) was one of the four traditional "Fathers of the Church". His Latin translation of the Bible is known as the *Vulgate.*

The sepulchre of the children of Israel. See Matthew 2.16. WW writes, "On the other side of the chapel is another grave, where many of the bodies of the Innocents slain by Herod were thrown."

It is seven miles from Bethlehem to Mount Judea. WW says, "One travels four miles northwest from Bethlehem to the mountains of Judaea."

A chapel where St John was beheaded. The execution of St John the Baptist is described in Matthew 14.10. In Josephus, *(Antiq.* XVIII. v.2), in a passage of doubtful authenticity, the place of his imprisonment and death is given as the fortress of Machaerus by the Dead Sea. He was believed to have been buried at Sebaste in Samaria.

87. The cliff which opened by itself where he was hidden. The story of how St John the Baptist, as an infant, was saved from Herod's men is to be found in the *Protoevangelion,* 16.3-7, "And instantly the mountain was divided and received them". For failing to reveal the whereabouts of his infant son Zacharias was murdered, (see note 74). WW's account in his Chapter 7 is very similar.

88. Where Our Lady composed the *Magnificat.* WW and his group also visited this site. The meeting of Mary and Elizabeth in the house of Zacharias, at which the babe leaped in Elizabeth's womb and she greeted the BVM as the mother of the Lord, is known as the "Visitation". In reply Mary sang the *Magnificat,* as described in Luke 1.39-55. From early times this was the canticle of Vespers in the Western Church and it appears in Evensong in the *Book of Common Prayer.*

A well where Elizabeth washed St John's clothes in childhood does not appear in WW.

89. A church where St John Baptist was born. WW adds some picturesque detail, "On the

right hand side is a church where the Saracens keep their animals. The entrance to the chapel is on the north side. On its eastern side is an altar on the spot where St John the Baptist was born." Luke 1.57 mentions the Baptist's birth.

90. Four miles from Mount Judaea on the road to Jerusalem is a church where a tree of the Holy Cross grew. There was great interest in the Middle Ages in the Cross, which was a fruitful source of relics, some of them tiny. The story of the Invention and Exaltation of the True Cross is to be found in *The Golden Legend*. The best known cycle of paintings illustrating it is that by Piero della Francesca in the Basilica of San Francesco, Arezzo, which was painted between 1452 and 1459, i.e. at the very time RL was making his pilgrimage.

According to tradition the tree grew from a seed from the Tree of Sin, planted in the dead Adam's mouth by his son, Seth. It grew until the time of Solomon, who cut it down to build his Temple. The craftsmen rejected it and used it as a bridge over the stream, Siloam. When she visited Solomon the Queen of Sheba had a vision about the bridge which foretold that it would be used for Christ's Cross. She declined to cross it and Solomon had it buried deep in the earth.

One tradition says that the Cross was made of four varieties of wood, one from each quarter of the world. In the Church of the Nativity in Bethlehem WW was shown "a small hole, about half an ell deep and more than half a foot wide where it is said that a dry, barren tree once stood. At the time of the Nativity it flourished and was green and formed one of the timbers of Christ's Cross."

While returning to Jerusalem, WW was shown "closer to Jerusalem, in a valley on the left, the Monastery of the Holy Cross, where Gorgians minister. Behind and beneath the high altar is a ditch where the wood of the Holy Cross grew". This is probably the "church" here mentioned by RL.

91. Pilgrimage of Bethany. See note 76 on Pilgrimages. WW gives a similar heading.

A temple where St Lazarus was buried. Lazarus was the brother of Martha and Mary. WW writes of this site, "In Bethany the first site is an old castle in which is a fine tomb of St Lazarus whom Christ raised from the dead."

92. A small chapel where Christ stood when he raised Lazarus from death to life. The raising of Lazarus is described in John 11.43 and 44. Of his subsequent life nothing is told in the New Testament. Tradition has it that he, with his sisters and friends, was put in a leaking boat by the Jews and miraculously reached Cyprus where he became bishop at Kition. In 890 his supposed relics were translated to Constantinople where a church was built in his honour by Leo VI. In the 11th century the legend spread in the West that he had been bishop of Marseilles and martyred under Domitian. The *Peregrinatio Etheriae* describes a procession to Bethany on the Saturday before Palm Sunday to the church erected over his tomb.

You will pay a fee of three shillings. For "entry fees" and the value of the shilling see notes 45 and 84.

The house of Simon the leper where Christ forgave Mary Magdalene her sins. From early times the woman who poured very precious ointment over Christ's head from an alabaster box in Simon's house, (Matthew 26. 6-13 and Mark 14. 3-9) was identified with Mary, the sister of Martha (John 11.2), and also the woman "which was a sinner" whose sins were forgiven (Luke 7. 36-48).

"Lord, had ye been here, Lazarus, my brother, had not been dead." Martha's reproach is recorded in John 11.21.

93. The house of Martha, where Christ often rested, is a little further on with the house of Mary Magdalene. WW says, "The house of the holy women, namely Martha and Mary, was there as well." i.e. WW says that there was one house while RL claims there were two.

94. Mount Quarantal. The temptation of Christ in the wilderness is described in Matthew 4.1-11; Mark 1.13 and Luke 4.1-13. The Greek Orthodox Monastery of the Temptation on Mount Quarantal (from *Quarantena* i.e. a period of 40 days) marks the site.
Christ fasted 40 days. See note above.

The devil showed Him all the riches of the world. Matthew 4. 8 and 9 and Luke 4. 5-7 describe this temptation.

St John baptised Christ. The description of the Baptism of Christ may be found in Matthew 3.13-17; Mark 1.9-11; Luke 3.21-22. See also John 1.32.

95. "The River Jordan runs west into the Dead Sea." A curious statement because the Jordan runs almost due south into the Dead Sea.

Sodom and Gomorrah were stricken and destroyed. According to Genesis 19.24 these two "cities of the plain" were destroyed by fire from heaven for their wickedness. Their fate was proverbial and is mentioned in Matthew 10.15 .

96. Everyone has to pay the Sultan two Venetian groats. WW gives a great deal of information in his Chapter 1 about currencies in use at this period and rates of exchange. He says that there are 15 groats to the Venetian ducat and eight *soldi* (shillings) to the groat. From RL's statement here one can see the value of the pilgrim traffic to the Saracen rulers of Jerusalem. If each pilgrim had to pay two groats (16 shillings) as a personal fee to the Sultan and, since a pilgrim galley carried, in round figures, 100 pilgrims, the Sultan obtained between 13 and 14 ducats (£80) as his share each time a galley reached Jaffa. To gauge the value of this one may recall the return boat fare for a pilgrim from Venice to Jaffa, including meals at the captain's table, was 40 ducats. The cost of a bed and bed linen at Venice was three ducats. See note 27.

In 1462, at the end of his second pilgrimage to the Holy Land, WW writes, "We were in the Holy Land for 13 days. We paid the Saracen chiefs 15 ducats for our safe-conduct over this period. A new chief, however, had been sent by the Sultan to govern the city of Jerusalem, and my *patronus*, Andrew Morason (Andreas Morosini), was delayed two days ashore at Jaffa until he paid the new lord of Jerusalem 50 ducats. In addition there was a war at that time between two Sultans, those of Babylon and Damascus, for control and power over the Holy Land and to settle which of them should be the ruler there."

97. A city called Mantua where there is some of Jesus Christ's blood. According to legend a sample of the Holy Blood was brought to Mantua by Longinus (see note below). It is preserved in the church of Sant' Andrea in that city and shown to the faithful on Ascension Day. Its authenticity was settled by Pope Pius II (Pope from 1458 to 1464), who declared that it had miraculously cured him of gout.

Longinus's body lies there. Longinus is the name traditionally given to the soldier whose spear pierced Christ's side while He was on the Cross (John 19.34). The tradition can be traced to the apocryphal *Acts of Pilate*, one version of which, the apocryphal *Gospel of Nicodemus,* 7.8, records the name. It was also given to the centurion who was standing by the Cross and said, "Truly this man was the son of God". (Mark 16.39; Luke 24.17) WW says, "In Nuremburg is the whole point of the spear with which Christ was wounded. It is like a spear used for hunting boars. It is guarded by 24 lords, each of whom has a key to the casket in which the spear is kept." The history of the spear and its political importance over the centuries up to the present time has been the subject of much research. The current view is that the relic, while ancient, was not part of Roman military equipment.

98. An Abbey on Mount St Bernard. The Great St Bernard is the name of an Alpine pass from Switzerland into Italy. The famous hospice there was founded by St Bernard of Menthon (923-1008), who was canonized in 1681. It is served by Augustinian canons who provide help for pilgrims and others crossing the pass and who breed the large St Bernard dog trained to find travellers lost in the snow.

A thorn of Jesus Christ. See note 35 for the two thorns revered in Rhodes. The crown of thorns is mentioned in John 19.2. Tradition says that it was preserved originally in Jerusalem and moved later to Constantinople. In the 13th century it came into the possession of St Louis XI, King of France, who built the *Sainte Chapelle* (completed in 1248) in Paris to house it. According to other versions it was broken up, and pieces are now claimed to be preserved in other places.

The cheek-bone of Saint Bernard was revered because, according to the legend of the Lactation of the BVM, St Bernard of Clairvaux saw a vision of Our Lady in the cathedral in Speyer, and, in response to his cry, *Monstra te, mater,* "Show thyself O mother", she expressed milk from one of her breasts which splashed his cheek.

The Duchy of Savoy. Savoy emerged from the collapse of the Frankish Kingdom of Burgundy. The House of Savoy maintained its independence, first as a County from c. 1000 to 1416 and then as a Duchy from 1416 to 1714, when it was linked with the Kingdom of Sicily and, soon after, with the Kingdom of Sardinia.

PART 5 - Bibliography

Apocryphal New Testament, (London; Printed for William Hone, Ludgate Hill, 1820).

Azzopardi, Canon John, *The Order's Early Legacy in Malta: the Sovereign Military Hospitaller Order of St John of Jerusalem of Rhodes and of Malta* (Valetta; Said International, 1989).

Bandinel, B. ed. *The Itineraries of William Wey* (London; The Roxburghe Club, 1857).

Barnes, R. and Branfoot, C. eds. *Pilgrimage; the Sacred Journey* (Oxford; Ashmolean Museum, 2006).

Brommer, P. and Krümmel, A., *Klöster und Stifte am Mittelrhein* (Koblenz; Görres Verlag, 1998)

Brown, Rawdon, ed. *Calendar of Venetian State Papers 1205-1509; Vol.1.* (London; Longmans, Green, Reader and Dyer, 1864).

Butler's Lives of the Saints, 4 vols, ed.H. Thurston and D. Attwater (Aberdeen; Burns and Oates, 1956).

Cambridge Medieval History, (Cambridge; Cambridge University Press, 1911-1936).

Davey, Francis, *The Itineraries of William Wey* (Bodleian Library, 2010).

De Voragine, Jacobus, *The Golden Legend*, selected and edited by C. Stace (London; Penguin, 1998).

Kollias, Elias, *The Knights of Rhodes; the Palace and the City* (Athens; Ekdotike Athenon S.A., 1998).

Kollias, Elias, *The Medieval City of Rhodes and the Palace of the Grand Master* (Athens; Ministry of Culture Archaeological Receipts Fund, 1998).

Mitchell, R.J., *The Spring Voyage* (London; John Murray, 1965).

Newett, M.M., *Canon Pietro Casola's Pilgrimage to Jerusalem in the Year 1494* (Manchester; Manchester University Press, 1907).

Ohler, N., *The Medieval Traveller*, trans. C. Hillier (Woodbridge, Boydell and Brewer, 1989).

Oxford Dictionary of the Christian Church (ODCC), ed. F.L.Cross and E.A.Livingstone (Oxford; Oxford University Press, 1997).

Prescott, H.F.M., *Jerusalem Journey* (London; Eyre and Spottiswood, 1954).

Webb, Diana, *Medieval European Pilgrimage* (Basingstoke; Palgrave, 2002).

PART 6 - Index

A

Aachen 6, 7, 9,16–17, 39, 45
Aalter 39
Aare 47
Aarschot 6, 39
Accademia 9
Acheldemach 43
Adam 42, 55, 63
Airolo 48
Ala 6
Albania 10
Alexandria 46, 50
Alps 15, 48
Amadeus 46
Andermatt 48
Andernach 6, 15, 39, 45
Anna 42, 56, 58
Annemuiden 6
Antioch 50, 58
Antwerp 7
Apostles 12, 43–44, 57–60
Aquae Grani, see Aachen 45
Archipelagus 18
Archpoet, The 49
Arena 40
Arsholt, see Hasselt
Ascension, The 13, 59, 65
Assisi 9, 17
Assumption, The 57, 60
Athanasius 9
Augustinians 65
Austria, Duke of 7
Axtis, see Methoni

B

Babylon 64
Bacharach (Baghragh) 6, 15, 39
Baffa, see Paphos
Bailiff 39
Barbarossa, Frederick 45
Basel 6–8, 39, 46–47
Baths 39, 45
Bedding 8, 14, 51
Bede 50
Bellini 9
Bellinzona (Bylyson) 6, 40, 48
Benedictines 15
Bergheim (Berkin) 39

Bernard, Mt 13, 18, 44, 65
Bethany 11, 44, 59-60, 63
Bethesda (*Probatica Piscina*) 5,56
Bethlehem 11–12, 43–45, 59-63
Bible, The Holy 13, 44, 55–56, 62
Bingen 6, 14–15, 39, 46
Bischwiller 39
Blind man 43, 59
Bodleian Library 5
Bodrum 11
Bologna 9
Bonn 6, 39, 45–46
Boppard 6, 15, 39
Brabant 39
Brasca, Santo 15
Brescello 40
Bruges 6, 39
Burgo Lugano, see Lugano
Burgoforte (Burgo) 40
BVM 17–18, 45, 52, 58, 62, 65
Bylyson, see Bellinzona
Byzantium (Constantinople) 53

C

Caiaphas 42–43, 54, 61
Cairo 11
Calais (Calysse) 6, 14, 39, 45
Calvary 11, 41-42, 55
Cande (Candy, Herakleion) 10, 13, 18, 52
Carmelites 15
Casola, Canon 16, 49, 52, 54–55
Cassanamata 40
Cassiopi (Casopa) 10,41, 52
Castles 8, 39–41, 48
Caves 12, 43
Cedron 42
Cenere (Syndyr) 40, 48
Centre of the World 42, 55
Certosa di Pavia 8, 40, 49
Cetinje 52
Chalcedon 51
Charlemagne 45, 50
Chioggia (Cloge) 8, 15, 40
Christ 7, 10–13, 16–18, 39–45, 49, 51–52, 54-65,
Cleophas 41, 54
Coblenz 6, 15, 39, 46
Coel, King 50

Cologne 6, 8, 16, 39, 44–46, 48–49, 62
Common Prayer, The Book of 51, 62
Como 6, 40, 49
Compostella 5–7, 61
Constance, see Konstanz
Constantine 11, 41, 49–50, 53
Constantinople 11, 18, 45, 51, 53, 63, 65
Corbola (Corbula) 40
Corfu (Corfowe) 9–10, 14, 18, 41, 52
Corpus Christi 11
Council, General 7, 39, 46
Creeds 9, 43
Cremona 6, 15, 40, 49
Crete 13, 15, 18, 52
Croatia 15
Crocodile 10, 52
Crusaders 61
Cursull, see Korçula
Cyprus 9–11, 13–15, 18, 53, 63

D

da Canedo 15
Dalmatia 7, 15
Damascus 18, 64
Danelaw Middle English 5
David, King 61
Dead Sea 5, 44, 62, 64
Dendermonde (Dyndyrmont) 6, 39
Devil 44, 64
Diest (Dyste) 6, 39
Diocletian 51
Disciples 41–43, 54-55, 57-59
Doge 9–10
Dominicans 15
Donkey 12, 14–15, 41–42, 44, 53
Donkey-man 41, 43-44
Dormition, The 57, 61
Dover 6, 14, 39, 45
Drusus 46
Dubrovnik (Ragusa) 9–10, 18, 41, 51–52
Ducats 8, 10, 12, 14, 40-41, 50–51, 64
Dunkirk 6, 39
Durres (Dyrrachium, Durase) 9–10, 41, 52
Dyndyrmont, see Dendermonde
Dyste, see Diest

E

Elijah 61
Emmaus 11, 41, 54
Etheria 54, 63
Eton College 5, 13
Exeter College, Oxford 5

F

Faido (Feyte) 6, 40, 48
Fees 12, 14–15, 54, 60–61, 63
Felix V, Pope 46
Ferrara 46
Ferries 8, 45, 49
Feyte, see Faido
Flad, Count 11
Flanders 45
Flemish 6, 39
Flewlynge, see Flüelen
Florence 6, 17–18, 57
Flüelen 6, 40, 47-48
Franciscans 11–12, 15–16, 47–48, 52–54, 56, 60-61
François I 8

G

Gabriel, Archangel 58
Galicia 61
Galilee 43, 58
Galleys 7, 10, 12–13, 15, 52
Gardener 11, 42, 54
Gaunte, see Ghent
Genoa (Ien, Jen) 40
Germany 6, 9, 39, 45, 48
Gethsemane 11
Ghent (Gaunte) 6, 8, 14, 39
Golden Gate (*Porta Aurea*) 5, 42, 56
Golden Legend 58, 63
Golgotha 54
Gomorrah 44, 64
Good Friday 7, 9, 11, 41, 52
Gortyn 52
Göschenen (Grott) 6, 40, 48
Gospel of the Birth of Mary 56
Gotthard, Monastery, Mount, Pass 6, 40, 48
Gravelines (Gravenynge) 6, 39
Gravesend 6, 45
Greece 15

Greeks 43, 53, 61
Groats 12, 14, 41, 44, 64
Grott, see Göschenen
Gulke, see Julich

H

Hasselt (Arsholt) 6, 39
Hausenstein 47
Hebrew 6, 44, 56, 59–60, 62
Herakleion (Candia) 9, 41, 52
Herod 42, 45–46, 56, 59, 61–62
Hilarion 18
Holy Cross 42, 44, 55, 63
Holy Ghost 42–43, 60
Holy Innocents 16, 44, 46
Holy Land 5–7, 10–12, 14–16, 41, 57,
        60-61, 64
Holy Sepulchre 12, 54, 59
Hospenthal 48
Hospitaller, Knights 6, 11, 13, 52
Hostilia, see Ostiglia
Huns 46
Hvar (Lysme), 11,15

I

India 43, 61
Indulgence 6–7, 11–12, 41
Isaiah 43, 59, 62
Israel 39, 43–44, 46, 58, 62
Istria 9–10, 15, 51

J

Jacob 61
Jaffa 8–10, 12–15, 17, 41, 44, 50, 53, 64
James, King of Cyprus 11
Jarra, see Zadar
Jehoshaphat 57
Jephonias 60
Jericho 7, 44
Jerome 44, 62
Jerusalem 5–7, 11–12, 14, 16, 39, 41-45,
        54-61, 63-65
Jews 12, 42–43, 45, 55–57, 60, 63
Joachim 42, 56, 58
Jordan 5, 7, 44, 60, 64
Joseph of Arimathaea 53
Judas 43, 57

Judea, Mount 44, 62
Julich (Gulke) 39, 45

K

Kempten 6
Kings of Cologne, see Magi
Kition 63
Konstanz 7
Korçula 9, 41, 51

L

Lamb, Paschal 60
Latin 5–6, 8, 10, 44, 46–47, 50, 62
Lausanne 7, 46
Lauterbourg 39
Lazarus 44, 63-64
Leo VI, Pope 63
Leonardo da Vinci 49
Lepers 42, 44, 63
Lombards 5, 13, 39, 45, 49
Lombardy 6, 40, 44, 48
London 7, 13, 39, 45
Longinus 13, 18, 44, 49, 65
Lor (Loreo) 15, 40
Lucerne 6, 8, 40, 47–48
Lugano 6, 40, 49
Lydda 41, 53
Lysme (Hvar) 11

M

Maastricht 6-8, 39
Maestro (Maestrale) 7
Maggiore, Lake 49
Maghlyn, see Mechelen
Magi (Kings of Cologne) 16, 45, 48, 62
Magnificat 44, 62
Mainz (Mens) 6, 8, 39
Malchas 9, 17
Mallasetum (Malmsey) 52
Malopero, Doge Pascale 9
Malta 52
Mantua 13, 18, 44, 65
Marckolsheim 39
Marseilles 63
Martha 44, 63-64
Martin, Pope 46
Mary Magdalene 42, 44, 54–55, 63-64

Marys, The Three 42, 55
Mass 12, 43, 60, 62
Maundy Thursday (Skyr) 17, 53, 60
Mauro, Doge Christophero 9
Maxentius 53
Mechelen (Maghlyn) 6, 39
Memmingen 6
Mens, see Mainz
Merano 6-7
Methoni 9-11, 14, 17–18, 41, 52
Metz 7
Michael, Archangel 49, 60
Milan 6, 8, 16, 40, 45–46, 49
Miles
      Dutch 6, 15, 39–40, 47
      English 6, 15, 39–40, 49
      Flemish 6, 39
      German 15
      Italian 6
      Lombard 6, 40
      Welsh 53
Milvian Bridge 53
Minos, King 52
Modyn, see Methoni
Money 9–10, 12–14, 39, 45, 52
Montenegro 52
Morea 11
Morosina 9, 13
Morosini, Andreas 14, 64
Moselle, River 7, 15, 39, 46
Moses 17
Mountford, Lord 16

N
Nahe, River 14–15, 39, 46
Nails 39–40, 42, 49, 55
Newcastle, Duke of 5
Newport 6, 39
Nicodemus, Gospel of 56, 65
Nicosia 18
Nunc Dimittis 51
Nuremburg 18, 65

O
Odyngborghe, see Ostend
Olivet, Mount 43, 57–59
Olten 47

Oppenheim (Otmerton) 39
Orlando, see Roland
Ortell, see Aalter
Ostend (Odyngborghe) 39
Ostiglia (Hostilia) 15, 40
Ottmarsheim (Otmarton) 39

P
Padua 7
Palm Sunday 42, 56
Paphos (Baffa) 9–10, 53
Paris 48, 65
Passion 41–43, 52, 54, 58–59
Pater Noster 43, 58
Patroni 10
Pavia (Pawe) 6, 8, 15–16, 40, 49-50
Payments 14
Pellagia 43, 58
Pergine 7, 9
Perugia 9
Philistines 53
Piacenza 8, 15, 40
Piero della Francesca 63
Pilate, Pontius 8, 40, 42, 47, 53–55, 65
Pilatus, Lake, Mount 8, 47
Pilgrims 5–16, 43, 45-47, 49–50, 52-56, 58,
      60-62, 64-65
Pius, Pope 7, 13, 57, 65
Po, River 6, 15, 40, 49
Pool of Sheep, see Bethesda, *Probatica*
      Piscina
Poreç 9
Porta Aurea (Golden Gate) 5, 42, 56
Probatica Piscina (Bethesda) 5, 42, 56
Protoevangelion of James, The 56
Pula (Pola) 9–10, 41, 51

Q
Quarantina, Mt 44

R
Rachel 61
Ragusa (Arogosa), see Dubrovnik
Rama (Ramys) 12, 14, 41, 44, 53
Relics 6–7, 9, 11, 13, 16–17, 40, 45–46, 50,
      60-61, 63,
Remagen (Remagyt) 6, 39, 45

Resurrection, The 41–43, 54, 58
Reuss 47
Reyn, see Rhens
Rheinbach 45
Rhens (Reyn) 15, 39
Rhine 6–7, 14–15, 39, 46–47
Rhodes (Rodys) 9–11, 13–14, 17–18, 41,
     52-53, 65
Roland 10, 40–41, 49-51
Rome 5–7, 9, 13, 15, 17-18, 44, 46, 53, 62
Romney wine 52
Rovinj 9–10, 41
Rur 45

S

Saints
    Anastasia   10, 17, 18, 41
    Andrew   8, 13
    Apollonia   16, 39, 46
    Arsenius   18, 52
    Augustine   16, 40, 49
    Bernard   13, 18, 44, 65
    Blaise   10, 18, 48, 52
    Christina   9, 17
    Christopher   17, 50
    Clare   9, 17
    Dismas   13, 18, 54
    Elizabeth   44, 62
    Euphemia   10, 17, 40, 51
    Francis   9, 16, 17
    George   6, 16, 17, 18, 41, 50,
        53
    Gregory   17, 40, 50
    Helena   12, 16, 41, 42, 45, 50,
        53, 54, 55
    James the Greater   43, 61
    James the Less   54, 58
    John the Baptist   42, 44, 45, 62,
        64
    John the Evangelist   42, 43, 60
    Katherine   17, 41, 52
    Leo   17, 18, 41, 52
    Louis, King of France   65
    Mamas   18
    Mark   9, 12, 17, 40, 51
    Mary Cleophas   41, 54
    Mary Magdalene   42
    Mathias   9

    Matthew   12
    Nicholas   9, 17
    Paul   52
    Peter   9, 16, 17, 39, 41, 46,
        49, 53, 60
    Simeon   10, 17, 41, 51
    Stephen   42, 43, 57, 60
    Sylvester   11, 41, 53
    Theophilus   17, 40, 50
    Thomas   43, 60
    Titus   13, 18, 52
    Ursula   46
    Zacharias   16, 17, 40, 43 50, 59,
        62
    Zoyolus   10, 17, 18, 41, 51
Saladin 6
Salinis 18
Saltys 15, 39
Samuel 41, 53
Saracens 11–12, 51, 54, 60, 63
Savoy, Duchy of 44, 46, 65
Scourges 42, 54
Scuole 9
Sesule 9, 52
Sheba, Queen of 63
Siena 6
Sievernich 45
Simon of Cyrene 12, 55
Simon the leper 44, 63
Sinzig 45
Sirmium 51
Skyr, see Maundy Thursday
Sodom 44, 64
Solomon 42, 56, 63
Spain 43, 61
Speyer 6, 8, 13, 39, 46, 65
Spoleto 9, 17
Stalett, see Stellata
Stations 42, 55–56, 59
Stellata 40
Strasburg 6, 8, 39, 46
Sugar 52
Sultan 11–12, 14, 44, 64
Sursee (Surmare) 40, 47
Syloe 11, 43, 58–59
Sympere, see Bodrum
Syndyr 48
Syon 11–12, 16, 43, 59–60

Syria 14

T

Tarsus 45
Temple, The 11–12, 14, 41–42, 56, 58–59, 61, 63
Temptation 43, 57, 64
Thorn, Holy 11, 17–18, 41, 44, 52, 55, 65
Thrusse 8, 39-40, 47
Ticino 40, 49
Tiptoft, Sir John 7
Trapp, Mount 40
Trento 6–7
Trier 7, 9, 17
Turks 11, 13

U

Ulm 6, 46

V

Venice 6–17, 40–41, 49–51, 61, 64
Via Dolorosa 12, 55
Via Julia Claudia 7
Virgins, The 11,000 16, 39, 46
Viscontis 49
Visitation, The 62

W

Wallachia 11
Wassen (Waschyn) 40, 48
Wey, William passim
Whit Sunday 43, 60
Worcester, Earl of, see Tiptoft
Worms 6, 8, 39, 46

Y

York 53

Z

Zadar (Jarra) 9–10, 17-18, 41, 51
Zodiac 5